W9-AAZ-279

How Are Digital Devices Impacting Society?

Melissa Abramovitz

INCONTROVERSY

ReferencePoint
Press®

San Diego, CA

ReferencePoint Press®

About the Author

Melissa Abramovitz has been a freelance writer for over twenty-five years and specializes in writing non-fiction magazine articles and books for all age groups. She is the author of hundreds of magazine articles, more than forty educational books for children and teenagers, numerous poems and short stories, several children's picture books, and a book for writers, *A Treasure Trove of Opportunity: How to Write and Sell Articles for Children's Magazines*. She is a graduate of the University of California, San Diego, and the Institute of Children's Literature and is a member of SCBWI and the Working Writer's Club.

© 2015 ReferencePoint Press, Inc.
Printed in the United States

For more information, contact:
ReferencePoint Press, Inc.
PO Box 27779
San Diego, CA 92198
www.ReferencePointPress.com

ALL RIGHTS RESERVED.
No part of this work covered by the copyright hereon may be reproduced or used in any form or by any means—graphic, electronic, or mechanical, including photocopying, recording, taping, web distribution, or information storage retrieval systems—without the written permission of the publisher.

Picture credits:
AJPhoto/Science Source, 34
© James Akena/Reuters/Corbis, 30
© Jenna Blake/Corbis, 74
© B.S.P.I./Corbis, 66
© Rick Friedman/Corbis, 72
© Francois Glories/Reuters/Corbis, 48
© Jan Haas/dpa/Corbis, 50
© Marianna Massey/Corbis, 17
© Shannon Stapleton/Reuters/Corbis, 22
© Stringer/Iraq/Reuters/Corbis, 79
© Tarker/Corbis, 13
Thinkstock Images, 9, 28, 44, 57, 62

LIBRARY OF CONGRESS CATALOGING-IN-PUBLICATION DATA

Abramovitz, Melissa, 1954-
    How are digital devices impacting society? / by Melissa Abramovitz.
      pages cm. -- (In controversy)
    Audience: Grade 9 to 12.
    Includes bibliographical references and index.
    ISBN 978-1-60152-772-1 (hardback) -- ISBN 1-60152-772-1 (hardback) 1. Information technology--Social aspects--Juvenile literature. 2. Social media--Juvenile literature. 3. Digital media--Juvenile literature. I. Title.
    HM851.A247   2014
    302.23'1--dc23
                                                                    2014030686

Contents

Foreword

In 2008, as the US economy and economies worldwide were falling into the worst recession since the Great Depression, most Americans had difficulty comprehending the complexity, magnitude, and scope of what was happening. As is often the case with a complex, controversial issue such as this historic global economic recession, looking at the problem as a whole can be overwhelming and often does not lead to understanding. One way to better comprehend such a large issue or event is to break it into smaller parts. The intricacies of global economic recession may be difficult to understand, but one can gain insight by instead beginning with an individual contributing factor, such as the real estate market. When examined through a narrower lens, complex issues become clearer and easier to evaluate.

This is the idea behind ReferencePoint Press's *In Controversy* series. The series examines the complex, controversial issues of the day by breaking them into smaller pieces. Rather than looking at the stem cell research debate as a whole, a title would examine an important aspect of the debate such as *Is Stem Cell Research Necessary?* or *Is Embryonic Stem Cell Research Ethical?* By studying the central issues of the debate individually, researchers gain a more solid and focused understanding of the topic as a whole.

Each book in the series provides a clear, insightful discussion of the issues, integrating facts and a variety of contrasting opinions for a solid, balanced perspective. Personal accounts and direct quotes from academic and professional experts, advocacy groups, politicians, and others enhance the narrative. Sidebars add depth to the discussion by expanding on important ideas and events. For quick reference, a list of key facts concludes every chapter. Source notes, an annotated organizations list, bibliography, and index provide student researchers with additional tools for papers and class discussion.

The *In Controversy* series also challenges students to think critically about issues, to improve their problem-solving skills, and to sharpen their ability to form educated opinions. As President Barack Obama stated in a March 2009 speech, success in the twenty-first century will not be measurable merely by students' ability to "fill in a bubble on a test but whether they possess 21st century skills like problem-solving and critical thinking and entrepreneurship and creativity." Those who possess these skills will have a strong foundation for whatever lies ahead.

No one can know for certain what sort of world awaits today's students. What we can assume, however, is that those who are inquisitive about a wide range of issues; open-minded to divergent views; aware of bias and opinion; and able to reason, reflect, and reconsider will be best prepared for the future. As the international development organization Oxfam notes, "Today's young people will grow up to be the citizens of the future: but what that future holds for them is uncertain. We can be quite confident, however, that they will be faced with decisions about a wide range of issues on which people have differing, contradictory views. If they are to develop as global citizens all young people should have the opportunity to engage with these controversial issues."

In Controversy helps today's students better prepare for tomorrow. An understanding of the complex issues that drive our world and the ability to think critically about them are essential components of contributing, competing, and succeeding in the twenty-first century.

Digital Devices: The Good, the Bad, and the Ugly

O n September 20, 2013, twenty-one-year-old Kimberley Davis of Port Fairy, Australia, slammed into a bicyclist while texting and driving. She stopped 300 feet (91 m) away from the injured man and called emergency responders. However, she refused to help the victim, who seriously injured his back and had extensive cuts and bruises. The man required surgery and was hospitalized for three months. Davis told a law enforcement officer, "I just don't care because I've already been through a lot of bullshit and my car is, like, pretty expensive and now I have to fix it. I'm kind of pissed off that the cyclist has hit the side of my car."[1]

On April 14, 2014, Davis pleaded guilty to dangerous driving. She received a $4,500 fine and lost her license for nine months. The loss of her license seemed to affect her the most. On Facebook she posted, "This sucks!"[2] and other comments lamenting her fate. News services and social media users widely shared her comments, resulting in widespread outrage. For example, Chris Matyszczk of CNET wrote, "I fancy if I broke someone's back, I'd care. At least a little. But I confess that I am not Kimberley Davis."[3]

Debates About Digital Devices

The story highlighted international concerns about people texting or otherwise using a cell phone while driving. At the same time, it drew attention to ongoing debates about whether modern digital devices and their applications have turned many people into narcissists. Narcissists are self-absorbed individuals who care little or nothing about others. Many social and behavioral scientists argue that cell phones and social media like Facebook and Twitter have drastically increased the number of narcissists. For example, technology expert Richard Watson writes in his book *Future Minds*, "We think cellphones are connecting us, but they are turning us into a society of rude, impatient, narrow-minded, stressed-out, aggressive, and isolated individuals."[4]

Other experts have different ideas about the relationship between digital devices and narcissism. Some believe that people who are already narcissistic are more likely to abuse social media and digital devices. Others believe that people today are generally not more selfish than in other eras, and still others believe that trends such as permissive parenting are responsible for the perceived increases in narcissism rather than digital devices. Others, such as Appalachian State University psychology professor Shawn Bergman, point out that links between technology and narcissism do not prove that one causes the other. "I think people have made a causal connection between Facebook and higher levels of narcissism because they know this one highly narcissistic kid who is always on Facebook. They use this anecdotal evidence as proof that there is a link between the two and conclude that Facebook is breeding narcissism in our children,"[5] Bergman states on the website Discovery News.

"We think cellphones are connecting us, but they are turning us into a society of rude, impatient, narrow-minded, stressed-out, aggressive, and isolated individuals."[4]

— Author and technology expert Richard Watson.

Correlation Versus Causality

Indeed, many debates about the effects of digital devices concern the issue of causality versus correlation. *Causality* means one factor is proved to cause another. *Correlation* means two factors are re-

"I think people have made a causal connection between Facebook and higher levels of narcissism because they know this one highly narcissistic kid who is always on Facebook."[5]

— Psychology professor Shawn Bergman.

lated, but neither necessarily causes the other. The only way of proving causality is to design scientific studies that control for every variable except the one being studied. For example, to prove that social media use causes narcissism, scientists would have to show that narcissistic people were not that way until they became active on social media and that other changes in their lives were not responsible.

Controversies over whether and how digital technologies cause other social trends have also arisen. Heated debates have emerged about whether playing violent video games causes people to commit crimes, whether digital media make people less smart and more lazy, and whether Internet addiction is a real phenomenon. Although social experts and laypersons do not debate the fact that digital devices have changed society, controversies about the quality, quantity, causality, and consequences of these changes are widespread.

Why Does It Matter?

Cell phones, laptops, and tablets are everywhere, including classrooms, restaurants, airports, and movie theaters. Most people acknowledge that the changes associated with these digital devices are both positive and negative. On the one hand, these devices make communication, information gathering, shopping, entertainment, and many other aspects of everyday life easier and faster. Social media and cell phones spread news, allow people with common interests to interact, and rally people to help others when needed. On the other hand, terrorists and other criminals use digital devices and the Internet to commit crimes. Cyberbullying has led numerous people to commit suicide. Some people constantly text and play video games to the exclusion of interacting directly with people around them. Many people express frustration if they are unable to use their phones for short periods of time.

Social and behavioral experts are concerned that widespread overdependence on digital devices is leading to negative effects on mental and physical health, family life, education, and human

Shopping, information gathering, and connecting with friends and acquaintances have been enhanced by smartphones and other digital devices, especially when they are paired with social media and other online tools. But experts worry that such devices are fostering the growth of narcissistic behavior.

compassion. As education and technology expert Neil Postman writes in his book *Technopoly*, "Stated in the most dramatic terms, the uncontrolled growth of technology destroys the vital sources of our humanity. It creates a culture without a moral foundation. It undermines certain mental processes and social relationships that make human life worth living."[6]

Psychologists and sociologists are not suggesting that people give up the positive aspects of digital devices. As psychologist Larry Rosen writes in his book *iDisorder*, "We are way past the point of no return."[7] But many are emphasizing the importance of stepping

"For all the possibilities that communications technologies represent, their use for good or ill depends solely on people."[8]

— Google chairman Eric Schmidt and Google Ideas director Jared Cohen.

back and analyzing how these technologies affect one's life. If schoolwork remains unfinished because of time spent on social media, or if an individual cannot sleep because she keeps checking her phone, experts suggest it might be time to take control over one's technology use rather than being controlled by a smartphone. The book *The New Digital Age: Reshaping the Future of People, Nations, and Business* is one of many recent publications to point out that "for all the possibilities that communications technologies represent, their use for good or ill depends solely on people."[8]

Facts

- According to the US Department of Highway Safety, 71 percent of teens and young adults say they have composed and sent text messages while driving.

- Penalties for distracted driving vary by state. For example, in Alaska the penalty for texting or e-mailing while driving is $10,000; in Oregon, it is $500; in New York, $243; and in California $20.

- When Harrisburg College in Pennsylvania instituted a one-week ban on using social media, only 10 to 15 percent of the students honored the ban, showing that most are overly dependent on digital technologies.

What Are the Origins of the Digital Device Controversies?

Many of the controversies over the impact of modern digital devices stem from three major factors. These controversies erupted because digital devices changed many aspects of personal and social life with lightning speed. These controversies also arose because the increasing popularity of these devices and applications coincides with increases in learning disabilities, behavior problems, and mental illnesses in young people. In addition, people realized that along with the positive changes in convenience and social connectivity that the Internet and digital devices allow, these technologies also consume a tremendous amount of time and have a dark side as hunting grounds for thieves, bullies, and others with evil intentions.

Taking Over with Lightning Speed

Digital devices have changed the way people communicate, learn, are entertained, find romantic partners, do business, access money from banks, shop, and more—all in the span of a few years. Before the rapid rise of computers and the Internet, technological innovations typically changed only one or two aspects of culture and daily life at a time. For instance, the fifteenth-century invention of the printing press allowed books and newspapers to be printed rather than handwritten. This changed the ease with which written documents were produced but did not affect other aspects of daily living.

Other new technologies experienced slower public acceptance than modern digital devices and applications. When the telephone and television were first invented, it took many years for them to become accepted and widely used. This was partly because they were initially so expensive and partly because most people saw no need for them. Once the costs dropped and the technologies became more sophisticated and useful, more and more people began using them. For example, televisions became available in the 1940s but did not become wildly popular until the late 1950s through 1970s. In 1948 only .4 percent of American families owned a television set. By 1978 this had grown to 98 percent.

Sociologist and communications expert Everett M. Rogers wrote five books between 1962 and 2003 about how society gradually accepts technological innovations. Rogers found that regular patterns of gradual acceptance emerged until the Internet became operational in the mid-1990s. At that time, the acceptance patterns for new digital devices that used the Internet or had mobile applications changed drastically. Rogers wrote in 2003, "The Internet has spread more rapidly than any other technological innovation in the history of humankind."[9]

Statistics about Internet and mobile phone use corroborate this rapid acceptance. Between 2000 and 2010 the number of people connected to the Internet increased from 350 million to more than 2 billion. At the same time, the number of cell phone subscribers went from 750 million to more than 6 billion. Not only were the Internet and mobile phones accepted rapidly, but these technologies also affected more aspects of human life than ever before. In his book *Overconnected: The Promise and Threat of the Internet*, technology expert William H. Davidow explains, "The railroad, automobile, telephone, radio, and television all affected us but not as deeply and broadly—and not nearly as quickly."[10]

"The Internet has spread more rapidly than any other technological innovation in the history of humankind."[9]

— Sociologist and communications expert Everett M. Rogers.

Between 1998 and 2006, interconnectivity and other trends that are so familiar today took the world from traditional modes of communication and information gathering to the modern world of texts and tweets. In 1998 Larry Page and Sergei Brin founded the search engine Google, which brought the world of information to people's fingertips. The blog-publishing service Blogger debuted in 1999, leading to the onslaught of blogs that allow ordinary people to express their views to a worldwide audience. In 2003 MySpace became the first social networking site, followed by Facebook in 2004. After YouTube debuted in 2005, Internet users could upload and download videos on millions of topics in an instant. Today YouTube is one of the most popular vehicles for shar-

Workers prepare printed publications at a seventeenth-century print shop. The invention of the printing press made it possible to produce books and newspapers more quickly than when they were written by hand, but daily life did not immediately change with this invention.

ing news, cultural events, and personal videos. Twitter launched in 2006, starting the so-called microblogging trend that is now one of the most popular ways in which celebrities, politicians, and many others share news and promote various causes.

Smartphones Dominate

As fast as the Internet and its applications changed society, experts say the smartphone in particular is responsible for the fastest, most far-reaching lifestyle changes. "It is hard to think of any tool, any instrument, any object in history with which so many developed so close a relationship so quickly as we have with our [smart] phones,"[11] stated a 2012 *Time* magazine article. The first smartphone was invented in 1992 but was too far ahead of its time to really catch on. IBM engineer Frank Canova Jr. developed the idea and helped build the prototype for an 8-inch-tall (20 cm), 2.5-inch-wide (6 cm), and 1.5-inch-thick (4 cm) touch-screen device the company named the Simon. The Simon was a phone, could access e-mail and send faxes, and had calendar and camera features. However, its applications were limited by the fact that no Internet browsers had been developed yet.

In 1997 Ericsson Mobile Communications called its GS88A the first real smartphone with limited Internet-browsing capabilities. By 2001 several companies had produced upgraded smartphones like the BlackBerry. BlackBerry devices and similar smartphones sold well, but they were primarily popular among businesspeople. It was not until 2007 that Apple released the first iPhone that lured the general public into buying smartphones that combined features of computers, phones, cameras, GPS navigators, and media players and had the unlimited apps that are so familiar today. Apple sold 1 million iPhones in seventy-four days. Since that time, mobile Internet use has grown at a rate of more than 60 percent per year.

Smartphones are now the most popular types of cell phones. Because of their convenience and versatility, many people have allowed them to become constant, indispensable parts of their

"It is hard to think of any tool, any instrument, any object in history with which so many developed so close a relationship so quickly as we have with our [smart] phones."[11]

— *Time* magazine journalist Nancy Gibbs.

lives without realizing that being constantly connected might have some detrimental effects. Indeed, many technology and behavior experts believe that many of the trends and controversies associated with digital technologies are occurring because people have unquestioningly welcomed the onslaught of new devices and applications into their lives. In her book *Failure to Connect*, education psychologist Jane M. Healy writes, "Rather than mindlessly accepting 'change' as important and necessary for our children, we should begin by pausing and reflecting on the long-range personal and cultural implications of our new technologies."[12]

Young People and Technology

Much of the awareness about the drawbacks of modern technologies focuses on young people. This is partly because the younger generation has grown up with these technologies and comfortably accepts and integrates new applications and gadgets into their lives. Teens and young adults are also among the most visible examples of people constantly texting, using social media, and playing video games. Thus, some older adults are quick to blame these technologies when they see young people acting selfishly or bullying others.

Several experts believe that some of the controversies about digital devices stem from the tendency of older people to criticize younger generations. For instance, psychologist Sara Konrath of the University of Michigan contends that "there is a long history of older adults criticizing younger generations for ways in which they are different from them. Older adults often complain that youth today are selfish, irresponsible, and have no sense of shame."[13]

Indeed, the statement that "children now love luxury; they have bad manners, contempt for authority; they show disrespect for elders. . . . They contradict their parents, chatter before company . . . tyrannize their teachers"[14] sounds like it could have originated in twenty-first-century America. However, historians attribute it to the ancient Greek philosopher Socrates (469–399 BCE). Another quotation—"The

"Rather than mindlessly accepting 'change' as important and necessary for our children, we should begin by pausing and reflecting on the long-range personal and cultural implications of our new technologies."[12]

— Educational psychologist Jane M. Healy.

worst part is that they don't care what people—their mothers and fathers and uncles and aunts—think of them. They haven't any sense of shame, honor, or duty. . . . They don't care about anything except pleasure"[15]—also sounds like the things many people say about present-day teens and young adults. But this statement appeared in a 1926 article in the *Dallas Morning News*—many years before computers and cell phones were introduced. Thus, modern researchers are hastening to determine whether those who claim that digital devices have turned young people into narcissists or scatterbrains are simply blaming these devices for behaviors that are not unique to the twenty-first century.

A Fear of New Things

In a similar manner, some criticisms and controversies about digital devices result from the fear and mistrust of new things. Throughout history the development of many new technologies led to claims that these devices would be or were already responsible for social ills. For example, newspapers first became popular in the 1700s. At that time, the French statesman Guillaume de Malesherbes claimed that obtaining news from a printed page would socially isolate readers because it deprived them of the traditional practice of hearing the latest news in church. When reading novels first became popular in the mid-1700s, a 1749 article in *London Magazine* described this trend as "a cause of 'negligence and folly,' a 'non-entity' that only 'vulgar' people enjoy, a 'poison,' a 'casual disorder,' a 'national evil,' 'the reflection of our own weakness,' and a 'vicious affection.'"[16]

After motion pictures debuted in the early 1900s, many people also rushed to blame them for social ills. By the 1920s millions of people, including children, were frequently going to movie theaters. As the book *The SAGE Handbook of Media Studies* notes, "Growing delinquency, increases in pregnancy rates, and other issues focused researchers' attention on potential causes and socialization influences, such as the motion picture and its theaters."[17] Such concerns led the Motion Picture Research Council to obtain a grant from the Payne Fund in 1928 to study the effects of movies on people. The results, published in 1933, indicated that children

and adults learned from movies, had sustained emotional responses to movies, and sometimes confused what went on in movies with reality. The researchers also found that "high levels of movie attendance were associated with declining morals, delinquent behavior, lower intelligence, and a number of other factors."[18]

However, the researchers realized these findings did not necessarily mean that frequently going to movies had undesirable consequences. The findings could indicate that delinquent individuals with low intelligence and loose morals frequently go to movies. Unable to determine what the causative factors were, the researchers concluded that "there is no simple cause-and-effect relationship. . . . Movies do have an effect on children, but those children who are most attracted to the worst movies tend to be those with the most problems to begin with. . . . The same picture may influence different children in different directions."[19]

Blaming Technology

Other new technologies elicited the same types of accusations and prompted studies to determine whether the technologies or other

An iPhone user checks on a location with Google Maps. The iPhones introduced by Apple in 2007 connected consumers with features such as cameras, GPS navigators, media players, and all kinds of other applications.

Skepticism About Technological Innovations

One reason controversies about modern digital devices and their applications have emerged is that no one was prepared for the speed at which these technologies were accepted and have changed many aspects of daily life. Technological innovations were traditionally greeted with widespread skepticism that led people to gradually accept and integrate these devices into their lives.

The following are examples of technologies that were greeted with skepticism:

- Shortly before the debut of the telephone, an 1865 *Boston Post* editorial stated, "Well-informed people know it is impossible to transmit their voices over wires, and even if it were possible, the thing would not have practical value."
- A 1939 *New York Times* article saw no future for television, stating, "The problem with television is that people must sit and keep their eyes glued to the screen: the average American family hasn't time for it."
- In 1943 IBM chairman Thomas Watson said, "I think there is a world market for maybe five computers."
- In 1977 Ken Olson of the Digital Equipment Corporation stated, "There is no reason anyone would want a computer in their home."

Quoted in Christopher Cerf and Victor Navasky, *The Experts Speak*. New York: Villard, 1984, pp. 227–29.

Quoted in Peter Edidin, "Confounding Machines: How the Future Looked," *New York Times*, August 28, 2005. www.nytimes.com.

factors were responsible for various social ills. In the 1960s and 1970s, for example, increasing crime rates and social unrest led researchers to focus on the effects of television and violent movies on human psychology and behavior. Studies by psychologist Albert Bandura and others found that people, especially children, do tend to imitate behaviors, including violent behaviors, they see in movies and television. However, these researchers found that other factors, such as the attractiveness of the actors and the social history of individual viewers, strongly influenced the likelihood of later violent behavior.

Based on these results, the US surgeon general issued a report in 1972 stating, "Under some circumstances . . . watching violent fare on television can cause a young person to act aggressively . . . [but] the effect is small compared with other possible causes, such as parental attitudes or knowledge of and experience with real violence of our society."[20]

Similar debates about whether newer technological innovations cause various social ills emerge regularly. However, these controversies have become more intense and widespread in recent years. This is because modern technologies have altered every aspect of existence and allow people to interact day and night with faceless screen names around the world. As Northwestern University professor Ellen Wartella and University of Cincinnati associate professor Nancy Jennings write, "Concerns have been renewed and heightened because of the level of interactivity possible when playing computer games and using the communication features of the Internet."[21]

News Reports Trigger Concerns

Concerns about modern technologies have also intensified because of numerous news reports about disturbing new trends. During the 1990s, when hanging out in Internet chatrooms became popular, news articles made people aware that pedophiles were lurking behind false identities in these chatrooms and luring children and teenagers to meet them in person. In 1998 the US Department of Justice initiated a program to alert parents to the presence of Internet predators. Its report stated, "Computer technology has,

The Origins of the Internet

The growth of the Internet is at the heart of many controversies about modern digital devices. The Internet originated in 1969 with the US government's Advanced Research Projects Agency Network (ARPANET) project. The goal was to develop a secure worldwide communications network for the US military. A group of computer experts incorporated the ideas of the so-called Galactic Network and packet switches into the ARPANET system.

J.C.R. Licklider of the Massachusetts Institute of Technology (MIT) introduced the Galactic Network idea in 1962. He proposed electronically linking computers all over the world so people could share information. Lawrence Roberts of MIT advanced Licklider's idea in 1965. He used a telephone line to connect a computer in California to one in Massachusetts. Roberts realized, however, that telephone circuits would not allow high-speed computer networking. He thus consulted scientists who were developing packet switches, which group digital data into small blocks called packets. This allows faster data transmission.

Roberts and other scientists incorporated packet switches into the ARPANET project. The system was first used by the military and then to link government and university research centers so scientists could exchange information. It grew into the worldwide Internet that connects people everywhere.

in essence, provided online predators the opportunity to enter the homes and bedrooms of children who are using the resource to communicate with friends, play games, or learn about the world they live in."[22] Many parents became alarmed, and many forbade their children to use the Internet without direct parental supervision. Filtering software that allows parents to regulate the types of websites children visit then became available. But even with these types of tools, many people continue to accuse computers and the Internet of fostering moral decline and allowing criminals who promote pornography and related pastimes to flourish.

At the same time, debates emerged about whether the rising use of computers, cell phones, and the Internet caused dramatic increases in learning disabilities, attention deficit disorders, and mental illnesses among young people. For instance, the Centers for Disease Control and Prevention (CDC) reported that the rates of attention-deficit/hyperactivity disorder (ADHD) diagnosis increased by an average of 3 percent per year from 1997 to 2003 and an average of 5 percent per year from 2003 to 2011. Teachers and employers also started noticing that young people had increasingly short attention spans and were increasingly self-absorbed. For example, job performance coach Dani Ticktin Koplik stated in a *Forbes* magazine article that people ages twenty to thirty-two have difficulties getting jobs because they lack basic manners during interviews, show no consideration for others around them, and submit sloppy résumés they do not bother to proofread. In addition, Koplik blamed "their sense of entitlement [and] lack of deference to authority."[23]

Reports on numerous instances of Internet addiction were another catalyst that fueled debates about the effects of modern digital devices. For example, in July 2007 Michael and Iana Straw of Nevada were convicted of child neglect after officials discovered they spent all their time playing video games rather than feeding or caring for their eleven-month-old daughter and twenty-two-month-old son. In December 2011 another high-profile story about technology addiction occurred when an American Airlines crew booted actor Alec Baldwin from a plane after he refused to turn off his cell phone. Baldwin claimed his addiction to the game *Words with Friends* caused his behavior. The proliferation of clinics that treat technology addictions has added to the debates about this phenomenon.

Cyberbullying and Sexting

The widely publicized phenomenon of cyberbullying leading teens and young adults to commit suicide also led many people to wonder whether social media and other aspects of digital devices were responsible for creating narcissistic, amoral individuals. One case that triggered much debate occurred in 2006 when Lori Drew of Missouri harassed thirteen-year-old Megan Meier on MySpace to the point that Meier killed herself. Drew launched her vendetta against Meier after Meier and Drew's daughter Sarah had a falling-out. Drew was convicted in court of a federal crime, but the conviction was later overturned. However, the case led to new federal and state laws making online harassment a crime.

Widespread coverage of sexting trends also fanned controversies over the effects of digital devices on society. Sexting involves sending sexually explicit messages or photos between smartphones. Surveys conducted in 2013 found that 49 percent of US adults participate in sexting. Percentages are even higher for adults ages eighteen to twenty-four. Many teens also participate in sexting, though different surveys have revealed widely disparate percentages.

Former US congressman Anthony Weiner (pictured in 2013) resigned after he used social media to send sexually explicit photos of himself to various women—and these photos became public. Sexting, as this practice is known, has provoked debate.

Numerous news stories about sexting provoked debate about related legal and moral issues. For instance, in 2011 sexting received much attention when New York congressman Anthony Weiner resigned after he sent sexually explicit photos to women other than his wife. Although this type of communication is legal for adults, debates emerged about whether sexting should be considered illegal pornography. Other news reports about teenagers who killed themselves after other teens shared sexually explicit photos of them and reports about teens being charged with child pornography for sexting photos and videos also fueled debate. In April 2013, for example, three Fairfax, Virginia, teens were charged with child pornography and faced prison terms of up to twenty years, plus being required to register as sex offenders, after they shared cell phone videos of drunken sex acts with other teens.

These types of incidents have led many states to pass laws allowing leniency for teens who sext, but Virginia has not. This resulted in many people demanding new laws in states like Virginia. Some lawmakers, however, are reluctant to pass laws that might allow pedophiles who engage in child pornography to evade harsh punishment.

Intensifying Debates

The debates over these types of issues have intensified because smartphones and other mobile devices have allowed people to access virtually any type of information and to instantaneously communicate anytime, anyplace. In turn, many people have noticed that this always on, always accessible capability has heightened trends indicating that people are increasingly impatient and intolerant of anything that does not happen instantaneously. As a 2013 *Boston Globe* article states, "Smartphone apps eliminate the wait for a cab, a date, or a table at a hot restaurant. Movies and TV shows begin streaming in seconds. But experts caution that instant gratification comes at a price: It's making us less patient."[24] A 2012 study at the University of Massachusetts, Amherst, revealed that Internet users became impatient when having to wait more than two seconds for a video to load. Twenty-five percent gave up and left the site after five seconds; fifty percent left after ten seconds of waiting. This impatience has translated to other aspects of life as well. More and more people are demanding same-day delivery of products and are willing to pay for things like special passes at Disneyland so they will not have to wait in line.

Another reason the digital device debates have intensified is that research that seeks to answer questions about what is going on and what is responsible often yields conflicting results. For example, research by psychologists Jean M. Twenge and W. Keith Campbell shows that the incidence of narcissistic personality traits in young people has risen dramatically since the Internet and mobile technologies became available. Yet studies conducted by psychologists Kali H. Trzesniewski and M. Brent Donnellan have concluded that "today's youth seem to be no more egotistical than previous generations. . . . In fact, today's youth seem to have psychological profiles that are remarkably similar to youth from the past 30 years."[25]

Since definitive answers to these types of questions have not yet emerged, many people have chosen to simply continue using digital devices in the manner in which they are accustomed. However, many others have begun to examine whether their use of these devices is excessive. This is exactly what most experts recommend. In the midst of the technology storm that so quickly changed so many aspects of society, these experts hope that people will simply slow down enough to analyze how they can enjoy the benefits without suffering the pitfalls.

"Smartphone apps eliminate the wait for a cab, a date, or a table at a hot restaurant. . . . But experts caution that instant gratification comes at a price: It's making us less patient."[24]

— *Boston Globe* journalist Christopher Muther.

Facts

- Wireless technologies are based on the work of the English chemist Michael Faraday. In the 1840s Faraday proved that electromagnetic currents could travel through air, with no need for an electrical wire, if started by a nearby moving magnetic field.

- In 1866 the American dentist Mahlon Loomis transmitted the first-known wireless signal between a kite connected to an electric meter on a mountaintop in Virginia to a second kite connected to a meter on a second mountain.

- Current wireless technologies use radio, cellular, satellite, and infrared transmissions of information from one point to another without using physical wires.

- According to Internet Live Stats, in 1993 there were 130 websites. By 2013 there were more than 672 million websites.

- Facebook debuted in 2004. By 2012 it claimed to have more than 800 million users who spent 700 billion minutes per month on the site.

- YouTube claims its users upload a total of seventy-two hours of video per minute, making YouTube one of the most popular Internet sites.

- Smartphones first became wildly popular in 2007. By the end of 2013 there were 1.4 billion smartphones in use, according to Business Insider Intelligence.

CHAPTER TWO

How Are Digital Devices Impacting Privacy and Social Interaction?

One of the most visible ways in which digital devices have changed the world is in how people communicate and share information. Before computers, modems, the Internet, and cell phones became popular, people could communicate face-to-face, send a telegram, send traditional mail, or call on a phone hooked by wires to the phone system. Ironically, while it has become easier and faster to stay connected through e-mail, instant messaging, texting, and wireless phones, some studies indicate that these devices may be increasing social isolation. They are also threatening the personal privacy that most people value.

Always Connected

A 2013 Pew Research Center study found that smartphones and other mobile devices that allow people to connect at all times have affected communication habits more than any other digital technologies. Although some individuals impose limits on this connectivity, many do not. The constant connection to jobs, friends, family, and the wider world has led many people to compulsively check texts, social media, and other online sites or use their cell phones while driving, dining, and even walking down the street.

Teenagers and adults under age fifty have plunged into this 24/7 connectivity more than any other age group. The Pew study notes that in 2006, 95 percent of teenagers had an online presence, but between 2006 and 2013 "the nature of teens' internet use has transformed dramatically . . . from stationary connections tied to desktops in the home to always-on connections that move with them throughout the day . . . and night."[26]

Studies find that this constant connectivity has led many people to prefer interacting through machines rather than face-to-face. A 2013 study found that 45 percent of the people surveyed admitted to texting, e-mailing, or phoning family members in the same house rather than talking in person. Rather than going to the store, many people prefer to order things online. Rather than going to the movies with friends, many people now stream movies on their laptops or tablets. Although for some people these changes are mainly timesavers, social and behavior experts find them worrisome for several reasons. One concern is that people who mostly interact electronically lose sight of what face-to-face interactions are all about. As Keith Davis of the US Department of Defense said in a 2012 report by the Pew Internet & American Life Project, "Social skills will be lost, and a general understanding of common sense will be a thing of the past."[27] Another concern is that when people interact primarily through texts and social media, they forget there are human beings with feelings on the other end. For instance, many people today break up with a boyfriend or girlfriend in a short text message or by changing one's social media profile status from *in a relationship* to *single*. While this may be quick and simple, it bypasses the interactive emotional elements that define relationships.

"Awash in technology, anyone can hide behind the text, the e-mail, the Facebook post or the tweet, projecting any image they want. . . . And without the ability to receive nonverbal cues, their audiences are none the wiser."[29]

— Susan Tardanico, a communications expert and the CEO of the Authentic Leadership Alliance.

People checking their cell phones, tablets, and computers at mealtimes—whether in homes or restaurants—has become commonplace. This is one example of how behavior has changed as a result of the profusion of digital devices.

When people interact face-to-face, they see body language and facial expressions and hear crying or laughing that reveal what the other person is thinking and feeling. When the only feedback is a brief text message, people have no idea how their words impact others. As communications expert Susan Tardanico explains in a *Forbes* magazine article, "Studies show that only 7% of communication is based on the written or verbal word. A whopping 93% is based on nonverbal body language. Indeed, it's only when we can hear a tone of voice or look into someone's eyes that we're able to know when 'I'm fine' doesn't mean they're fine at all."[28]

Overly relying on brief digital communications can sometimes have tragic consequences. For instance, in 2011 a college girl attempted suicide shortly after an upbeat texting session with her mother in which the girl said she was happy and doing great. The mother later found out her daughter had been depressed and had isolated herself in her dorm room. "Awash in technology, anyone can hide behind the text, the e-mail, the Facebook post or the tweet, projecting any image they want. . . . And without the ability to receive nonverbal cues, their audiences are none the wiser,"[29] Tardanico writes.

Even with these potential pitfalls, behavior experts do not believe it is necessary to abandon texts and similar ways of communicating. They do, however, caution that supplementing remote interactions with face-to-face ones is important.

Workplace Communications

The dynamics of business communications have changed along with those of personal communications. Some people now telecommute from their homes without having to drive to an office. Many people who work in offices also communicate mostly by e-mail or texting. These modes of interaction are so popular that many workers send a text or e-mail instead of walking five steps to speak with a colleague. In addition, many companies now conduct virtual meetings using Skype or conference calling instead of assembling in a conference room.

Although electronic interactions are convenient, many social experts are afraid the lack of face-to-face interactions is increasing social isolation in the workplace as well as in people's personal lives. Indeed, a 2010 survey of people who work in companies that conduct virtual meetings found that 66 percent said virtual meetings gave them a sense of isolation.

Many businesspeople have discovered that meeting in cyberspace can also be detrimental to teamwork and productivity. One survey respondent stated, "You need to connect with people. There is no way to connect with people virtually. . . . By experience, we have done in two days of face-to-face meetings what we could not achieve in two months [of electronic meetings]."[30]

As organizations and businesses recognize the potential pitfalls of no face-to-face contacts, some have addressed the issue by implementing e-mail–free days. For example, Intel, which makes computer chips, implemented e-mail–free Fridays in 2007. "E-mail isn't forbidden, but everyone is encouraged to phone or meet face-to-face. The goal is more direct, free-flowing ideas,"[31] explains a *USA Today* article.

The Positives of Remote Communications

Not everyone agrees that conducting business electronically is a negative thing. In the 2010 remote communications survey, one worker stated, "I find that remote working has more pluses than minuses. Focus is on tasks and deliverables, not on office politics." Another said, "Virtual teams often provide individuals with better quality of life, including ability to have flex hours to support a better work/life balance."[32]

In other situations, digital devices have brought newfound improvements to businesses in less-developed countries. For example, women in the Democratic Republic of Congo who support themselves through fishing used to catch fish each morning and bring the fish to the local marketplace. As the day went on, more and more unsold fish spoiled. Today, these women have cell phones. They catch fish and keep them tied to ropes underwater in a river until a customer calls in an order. Then they bring the fresh fish to the customer in the marketplace. This wastes fewer fish and reduces

A woman in the Democratic Republic of Congo shops for freshly caught fish. Fish sellers have reduced spoilage by taking orders from their customers by cell phone.

the chances that people will be sickened by eating spoiled fish.

Experts see nothing wrong with using digital devices for specific purposes such as selling fresher fish. But as with personal communications, concerns arise when remote communications push most or all face-to-face interactions aside. Even if e-mailing someone is faster and cheaper than visiting them, technology expert Richard Watson warns that "physical interaction is a basic human need and we will pay a very high price if we reduce all relationships (and information) to the lower-cost formats."[33]

The Connectivity Paradox

The "high price" Watson is referring to is isolation and shallow relationships. Social experts call the notion that connectivity and isolation can coexist the *connectivity paradox*. As an article in the *Atlantic* explains, "Within this world of instant and absolute communication . . . we have never been more detached from one another, or lonelier."[34] Studies indicate that more people than ever—over 60 million in America alone—say they are lonely. Some researchers blame modern technologies for this trend. For instance, a prominent 2006 study by sociologists Miller McPherson, Lynn Smith-Lovin, and Matthew Brashears concluded that Americans became more socially isolated after 1985 because the Internet and mobile phones weakened their social connections.

However, other researchers argue that digital devices strengthen social connections. A 2009 study by the Pew Internet & American Life Project was among the first to find that people who frequently use the Internet and mobile phones to communicate have larger and more diverse social networks. In addition, the study found that these people are more socially active and connected to their communities. The Pew study did not prove that frequent Internet and cell phone use causes people to have more diverse social networks; it merely indicated an association between the two.

More recent studies find that the ways in which people use technologies, rather than the technologies themselves, are responsible for creating isolation or improved social ties. For example,

"Within this world of instant and absolute communication . . . we have never been more detached from one another, or lonelier."[34]

— Journalist Stephen Marche.

Carnegie Mellon University researcher Moira Burke discovered that the effects of Facebook vary according to how individuals use the site. Whereas those who converse with friends report that Facebook makes them feel less lonely, those who merely click *like* or scroll past updates report feeling more lonely. In addition, University of Chicago neuroscientist John Cacioppo finds that balancing face-to-face interactions with digital communications makes a difference. "The greater the proportion of face-to-face interactions, the less lonely you are. The greater the proportion of online interactions, the lonelier you are,"[35] he states.

An Equal Voice

Other social scientists report that digital technologies can decrease isolation by giving a voice to those who previously would not have been able to reach a vast audience. People use blogs and social media to bring attention to injustice and to unite people in supporting others every day. People with mental and physical disorders and those facing difficult situations such as bullying often benefit from online support. At the same time, Internet users rally support for others in need. For example, the day after Facebook announced that users could post their organ donor status on their profiles in 2012, Donate Life America reported huge increases in organ donor registrations. California, for instance, saw a 5,000 percent increase and Minnesota a 12,500 percent increase.

"The greater the proportion of face-to-face interactions, the less lonely you are. The greater the proportion of online interactions, the lonelier you are."[35]

— University of Chicago neuroscientist John Cacioppo.

Technology experts Eric Schmidt and Jared Cohen state in *The New Digital Age* that they believe these communications opportunities will "help reallocate the concentration of power away from states and institutions and transfer it to individuals." They also state that rather than isolating people, "being connected virtually makes us feel more equal—with access to the same basic platforms, information and online resources."[36]

Privacy and Digital Communications

While controversies exist about whether modern technologies have increased social isolation, experts and laypersons agree that they have

Social Capital

Social capital refers to the notion that social ties and community activities are valuable and enhance both society and individuals' lives. Political scientist Robert Putnam writes in his book *Bowling Alone* that the social capital invested in clubs, religious organizations, and service organizations gradually decreased as watching television took up more and more of people's spare time after the 1960s. When time spent on the Internet, video games, and mobile technologies increased in the late 1990s, traditional community activism declined even more as people spent more of their leisure time alone with machines.

Putnam also acknowledges that social involvement historically waxed and waned as people adapted to new ways of becoming socially engaged through new technologies. He writes, "Perhaps the younger generation today is no less engaged than their predecessors, but engaged in new ways." The fact that many people today support others in online common-interest groups, launch crowdfunding drives, and rally searches for missing people or desperately needed organ donations via the Internet and social media supports Putnam's idea. People today may be building social capital in new ways, but this does not mean the modern era is devoid of social ties.

Robert Putnam, *Bowling Alone*. New York: Simon & Schuster, 2000, p. 26.

dramatically diminished privacy. According to Clark University professor Judith Wagner DeCew, humans have always valued and needed privacy: "Although not all societies protect privacy in the same way, in virtually every society individuals engage in patterns of behavior and adopt avoidance rules in order to seek privacy."[37]

Attitudes and laws about privacy have changed over time to keep pace with social and technological innovations. For instance, after the telephone became popular, the US Congress instituted laws governing wiretapping. However, many psychologists and sociologists are concerned that modern digital technologies have threatened privacy more than any other force in history. Now that many health, financial, and personal records are electronic, hackers and other unauthorized people have gained access to millions of private documents. This often results in identity theft, financial ruin, and other serious consequences. For example, the Office of Civil Rights of the US Department of Health and Human Services reports that the private electronic health records of nearly

A surgeon performs a kidney transplant. Organ donor registrations rose in 2012 after Facebook announced that users could post their organ donor status on their profiles.

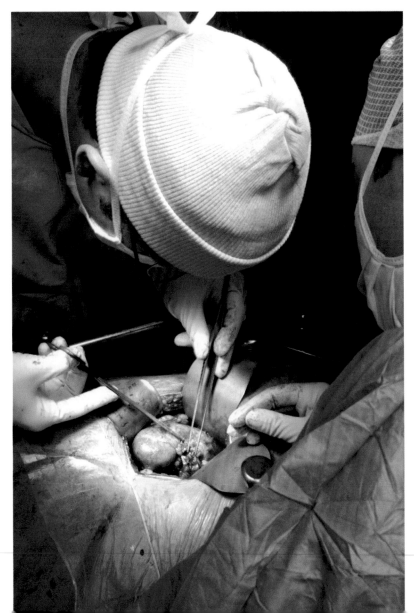

30 million people were breached between 2009 and 2013. This number includes breaches by hackers, unauthorized snooping in patient records by hospital employees, and accidental breaches due to carelessness.

Intrusions on privacy also occur when people post private information or photos about themselves or others online. The right to post information about others is protected by the First Amendment to the Constitution's right to free speech unless it involves threats or stalking. However, when private information can be shared easily worldwide, the embarrassment and harm from such postings can be emotionally devastating. In the past these types of privacy breaches mostly had affected celebrities, but in the age of cell phone photos, blogs, and social media, anyone can become instantly famous, even if he or she has no desire to be in the public spotlight.

Internet Shaming

A person's reputation can be ruined as quickly as online postings can go viral. In one widely publicized incident in 2005 in South Korea, a young woman's dog pooped on a subway train floor. The woman refused to clean up the mess. A fellow passenger shot a video of the incident with his cell phone camera and posted it online, where it spread like wildfire. Numerous bloggers then publicly identified and published details about the woman and her family. She was harassed to the point that she stopped going to college classes and lost her job. She also acquired the nickname "Dog Poop Girl," a name that might follow her for the rest of her life.

Before the cell phone and Internet age, the woman's fellow passengers might have told a few friends, and that would have been the end of it. But with Internet sharing, the incident forever changed the woman's life. Although people who viewed the video believed her actions were inconsiderate, many questioned whether she deserved to be publicly humiliated or lose her job. According to the the *Washington Post*, debates arose about "whether the Internet mob had gone too far."[38]

Social theorists have different views about how digital technologies have changed public shaming practices in cases like the Korean subway incident. Privacy expert Daniel Solove of George

Washington University states that the incident showed how bloggers are acting "as a cyber-posse, tracking down norm violators and branding them with digital scarlet letters."[39] Other experts point out that the Internet has merely given people a convenient method of publicly shaming those who in earlier eras would have been put in a stockade in the town square. Most experts, however, agree that the damage done by worldwide exposure is more extensive than previous public shaming achieved.

Governments are tapping into the power of Internet shaming by posting lists of people who have not paid their taxes. Similar postings have been used to humiliate so-called deadbeat divorced parents who refuse to pay court-ordered child support. As a result, numerous US states have collected millions of dollars in taxes and have reported that some deadbeat parents have started to fulfill their obligations. Thus, advocates of this practice believe it is an efficient method of encouraging compliance with the law.

Opponents believe the potential for harming the reputations of innocent people makes the government's use of Internet shaming unethical. As Pete Sepp of the National Taxpayer's Union states in a *USA Today* article, "How are people going to be compensated when, inevitably, mistakes are made?"[40] One widely publicized mistake occurred in 2014. Maria Borrallo, the nanny of the British prince George, was named on a tax-shaming website in her native country of Italy. She had paid what she owed, but her name mistakenly remained on the list. A friend of Borrallo's told the Scottish newspaper *Daily Record*, "It's a major source of embarrassment to her . . . but there's nothing she can do about it."[41]

Oversharing

Experts are also concerned about the tendency of many people—especially young people—to share information about themselves online without regard for the possible consequences. This phenomenon is called oversharing. A 2012 report by the McCann Truth Central technology consulting company states that several forces have spurred oversharing. One factor is that the Internet has broken down many of the previous borders that separated people in different areas of the world. The ability to communicate with people all

Oversharing and Emotions

Wharton Business School marketing professor Jonah Berger has done a great deal of research on what makes people overshare information about themselves on the Internet. His studies indicate that oversharing is most likely to occur when someone is experiencing strong emotions. One study showed that when people view videos that provoke strong emotions, they are more inclined to want to share other types of information with others. These and similar findings led social psychologist Kim Peters to conclude that "what we share may have as much to do with the stimulation provided by the environment as with the information itself."

No one knows why emotional stimulation provokes the urge to share. Psychologist Mark Schaller of the University of British Columbia hypothesizes that "perhaps there is a natural tendency to share information and the social inhibitions that get in the way are reduced under conditions of arousal." However, scientific studies have yet to prove this or other theories that might explain Berger's findings.

Quoted in Hans Villarica, "The Physiology of (Over-)Sharing," *Atlantic*, August 5, 2011. www.theatlantic.com.

over the world has led many individuals to tear down the borders that used to separate private from public life. In a similar manner, the fact that average people can now follow celebrities through Twitter and other social media has led to the impression that the daily minutia of most anyone's life will be equally thrilling to others.

Another factor is that television reality shows like *Hoarders* and *Wife Swap* have made it acceptable for the public to view intimate details of a person's everyday life. Coupled with the ease of posting online photos, videos, and status reports, experts believe reality shows have spurred many people to lose their inhibitions about oversharing information about themselves or others on social media. A 2013 *Huffington Post* article calls the world of social media a "global orgy of oversharing" and notes that "it is easy to begin with the cute and to step into the gross or invasive."[42] For example, many people begin posting cute pictures of their new babies and later fail to realize that no one wants to see pictures of the children being potty trained or receiving stitches at the hospital. In a similar manner, people progress from posting regular photos of themselves to sharing nude selfies with strangers.

Researchers have discovered that people are most likely to overshare when they are experiencing intense emotions of any type, including joy, anger, fear, or sadness. The fact that intense emotions can get in the way of rational thought may help explain why many people do not consider the consequences of oversharing. For instance, many people excited about an upcoming vacation post where they are going and when. Thieves who peruse social media sites then read the postings and rob the vacationers' homes while they are away.

"People have really gotten comfortable not only sharing more information and different kinds, but more openly and with different people."[45]

— Facebook CEO Mark Zuckerberg.

A seventeen-year-old girl in Australia made a Facebook posting that had equally bad consequences. She posted photos of large amounts of cash as she helped her grandmother count her savings. Seven hours later two thieves robbed the home of the girl's parents of cash and personal property. They did not realize that the girl no longer lived at home, and they believed the cash pictured online was at her parents' house.

In another oversharing case, a teen accidently shared a Facebook posting about her birthday party with the public. She received twenty-one thousand RSVPs, and the guests who showed up trashed her family's home. Teenager Lane Sutton, who works as a social media coach, recommends frequently checking social media privacy settings and turning off location apps like *We Know What You're Doing* and *Girls Around Me* to avoid these types of problems. Sutton also writes, "If you feel the need to share online, don't say something you wouldn't say offline."[43]

Attitudes About Privacy

Oversharing has led to the view that many individuals no longer value privacy. Oxford University neuroscientist Susan Greenfield, for example, has written extensively about her perception that "privacy appears to be a less prized commodity among the younger generation of 'Digital Natives': apparently 55 percent of teenagers have given out personal information to someone they don't know, including photos and physical descriptions. . . . It has become more important to have attention, to be 'famous.'"[44]

With a bird's-eye view of the world of social media, Facebook chief executive officer (CEO) Mark Zuckerberg agrees that attitudes about privacy have changed, stating, "People have really gotten comfortable not only sharing more information and different kinds, but more openly and with different people. That social norm is just something that has evolved over time."[45] Zuckerberg believes that even though many people on Facebook and other social media sites can determine their own privacy settings, many seem unconcerned when their postings are shared with friends of friends of friends. However, many Facebook users and social media experts have challenged the viewpoint that attitudes about privacy have changed drastically. In fact, in 2012 the US Federal Trade Commission took Facebook to court because so many customers complained that Facebook deceived them by forcing them to share more information than they were aware was being shared.

Experts such as Irina Raicu of the Markkula Center for Applied Ethics have also challenged the notion that people no longer value privacy. Raicu writes, "Although it may be true that people are now 'sharing more information and different kinds,' many are now also trying to regain control over who has access to that information, and for what purposes."[46] She points out that more than 80 percent of Internet users who use social media choose privacy settings that do not allow the public to view their postings. Many people also use software that prevents oth-

"Although it may be true that people are now 'sharing more information and different kinds,' many are now also trying to regain control over who has access to that information, and for what purposes."[46]

— Irina Raicu, director of the Markkula Center for Applied Ethics.

ers from tracking their activities. In addition, the 2012 McCann Truth Central study found that 75 percent of people throughout the world worry about the loss of personal privacy that goes along with the Internet. These types of data show that most people still value privacy. As with other issues concerning the social changes related to modern digital devices, awareness of how these devices threaten privacy is growing, and solutions are being pursued.

Facts

- A 2013 Pew Research Center study found that 78 percent of teens in the United States have a cell phone, 37 percent have a smartphone, and 74 percent access the Internet on a cell phone, tablet, or other mobile device.

- Many people, especially young people, communicate primarily by texting. In 2010 teenager Allison Miller told the *New York Times* that she typically sent and received more than twenty-seven thousand texts per month.

- A 2011 survey by the Pew Internet & American Life Project found that 13 percent of cell phone users admit that they pretend to be using their phone to avoid interacting with people around them.

- A 2014 Nielsen report indicates that the average American spends more than sixty hours per week on digital devices, leaving little time for face-to-face interactions.

- A 2010 *Consumer Reports* study found that 52 percent of social media users post risky information online.

- According to a *Huffington Post* article, Internet shaming of people and businesses that do not pay their taxes resulted in the state of California collecting $27.9 million in 2011 alone.

How Do Digital Devices Affect the Brain and Thought Processes?

S cientists have evidence that, in addition to changing the ways in which people communicate and gather information, modern digital devices also change the human brain. These brain changes may, in turn, affect how people learn, work, and function. Some experts believe these brain changes are undesirable and uniquely result from modern technologies. Others see the changes as positive, and still others emphasize that any type of experience or learning causes similar brain changes.

Neuroplasticity

The ability of neurons (nerve cells) in the brain to alter their connections in response to learning or experience is known as neuroplasticity. Doctors and scientists study brain activity generated by these connections using an imaging technique called functional magnetic resonance imaging (fMRI). FMRI is a specialized type of MRI that uses magnets and radio waves to measure oxygen flow in the brain's blood vessels. This oxygen flow reveals which areas of the brain are active at a given time.

Many fMRI studies have shown that brain activity and structure change from exposure to stimuli or other experiences, including digital technologies. Research by Gary Small at the Semel Institute for Neuroscience and Human Behavior at the University of California, Los Angeles (UCLA), indicates that although the brains of children and teenagers are most easily changed by technology, older people's brains also respond with neural rewiring. In one study Small found that adults ages fifty-five to seventy-six who frequently use the Internet show twice as much brain activity during Internet searches compared to adults who never use the Internet. In particular, they show more activity in the frontal, temporal, and cingulate cortex areas, which are involved in decision making and reasoning. Small believes that although many older adults experience declining brain function, using the Internet may represent a new way to keep the brain active. "A simple, everyday task like searching the Web appears to enhance brain circuitry in older adults, demonstrating that our brains are sensitive and can continue to learn as we grow older,"[47] he states in a UCLA Newsroom article.

> "Throughout human history, human brains have elastically responded to changes in environments, society, and technology by 'rewiring' themselves."[48]
>
> — University of Florida education technology professor Cathy Cavanaugh.

University of Florida education technology professor Cathy Cavanaugh emphasizes that this type of brain rewiring is not unique to modern technologies. "Throughout human history, human brains have elastically responded to changes in environments, society, and technology by 'rewiring' themselves. This is an evolutionary advantage and a way that human brains are suited to function,"[48] she explains in a 2012 Pew Internet study.

Although the brain changes from any experience to some degree, studies by neuroscientist Daphne Bavelier at the University of Rochester indicate that different experiences and different technologies lead to different types of changes. Bavelier explains, "As with food, the effects of technology will depend critically on what type of technology is consumed, how much of it is consumed, and for how long it is consumed."[49]

Bavelier also finds that the intent of a particular technology—be it education or entertainment—may not affect a user's brain and behavior accordingly. "Some products designed to benefit cognitive development actually hinder it, while some products designed purely for entertainment purposes lead to long-lasting benefits,"[50] she states.

Brain Changes from Video Games

Bavelier and other researchers find that video games, which are designed for entertainment, can lead to beneficial brain changes. Bavelier's research shows that playing action video games improves attention, the ability to notice small details about pictures, eye-hand coordination, and speed. Skilled video gamers also perform better than nongamers when they multitask. Other studies indicate that video gaming can increase brain size and enhance certain brain connections. A 2013 study at the Max Planck Institute for Human Development in Berlin found that video gaming stimulates the growth of new neurons and forges new connections in the gray matter (parts of the brain that house neuron cell bodies) in the right hippocampus, right prefrontal cortex, and cerebellum. These areas of the brain govern memory, strategic planning, and spatial orientation (the sense of direction). Gamers who report that they enjoy playing video games the most show the most brain growth. Lead researcher Simone Kuhn notes in a *Psychology Today* article that "while previous studies have shown differences in brain structure of video gamers, the present study can demonstrate the direct causal link between video gaming and a volumetric brain increase. This proves that specific brain areas can be trained by means of video games."[51] The researchers believe these findings might help psychiatrists treat mental disorders like schizophrenia and Alzheimer's disease, which involve a loss of nerve cells.

Neuroscientist Lauren Sergio of York University in Toronto, Canada, has used fMRI to discover that skilled video gamers also tend to use different parts of their brains than nongamers do. Skilled gamers mostly use the frontal cortex—an area involved in planning, multitasking, and attention—when performing tasks that require eye-hand coordination. Nongamers, on the other

Some researchers say that action video games improve attention, eye-hand coordination, and even stimulate brain growth. Other researchers believe brain changes resulting from frequent video game play are not so positive.

hand, mostly use the parietal cortex for these tasks. Sergio explains in a National Public Radio article that "the non-gamers had to think a lot more and use a lot more of the workhorse parts of their brains for eye-hand coordination. Whereas the gamers really didn't have to use that much brain at all, and they just used these higher cognitive centers to do it."[52]

However, other studies indicate that playing video games can lead to negative brain changes in some situations. One study by researchers in China found that adolescents who are addicted to playing video games show decreases in gray matter in the prefrontal cortex, anterior cingulate cortex, and cerebellum and in white matter in the hippocampus. White matter is composed of nerve fibers: the axons, or extensions, on neurons that communicate signals to other neurons. The amount of brain shrinkage was greatest in those teens who were addicted to video games the longest. All the areas that shrank are involved in behavior control and information processing. Since other studies indicate that people with Internet and gaming addictions are impulsive and do poorly in school, the Chinese researchers believe their study provides clues about why this is true.

The Effects of Excessive Screen Time

Studies on people who use the Internet excessively find results similar to those in the gaming addict study. One study found that people who use the Internet for more than ten hours per day have less gray matter than those who are online for less than two hours per day. A 2013 study by Chinese researchers determined that Internet-addicted adolescents also have an abnormally low number of connections between neurons in the cortex and subcortex. The cortex is primarily involved with thinking and reasoning, while the subcortex mainly coordinates emotions and sensory and motor functions with the cortex.

The connection patterns in Internet addicts are similar to those seen in people with other types of addictions, such as drug addictions. The researchers note that further research is needed to determine whether Internet and other addictions cause these abnormal connections or whether these brain features are responsible for making people vulnerable to addictive behaviors.

Even when people are not actually addicted to technology, many experts are concerned that overuse of digital devices may be changing the brain and human behavior in negative ways. Neuroscientist Susan Greenfield is one of the most vocal proponents of this viewpoint. Greenfield believes overuse of technology and the lack of interpersonal interactions that often go along with this overuse result in brain changes that impair people's independence and ability to think on their own. She writes in a *Telegraph* article that the end result may be that "the mind might remain more childlike, reactive and dependent on the behavior and thoughts of others."[53]

Many scientists and commentators disagree with Greenfield's opinion that technology is changing the human brain in over-whelmingly negative ways. Critics such as Australian neuroethi-cist Neil Levy point out that although Greenfield interprets the

Technology-Related Brain Changes May Be a Good Thing

Australian neuroethicist Neil Levy criticizes Susan Green-field's contention that the brain changes associated with modern technologies are all undesirable. Levy writes that new technologies throughout history have changed hu-man brains with positive results. For instance, when hu-mans began using written language thousands of years ago, this may have weakened their capacity to remember things because they could now rely partly on written in-formation to help them remember. However, the poten-tial loss of some degree of memory could also have had positive results. Levy explains:

> It may be that writing did not merely provide us with an external memory store that was superi-or to brain-based memory (much more reliable, for one thing). By decreasing the burden on our memory, it may also have freed up brain-based processing resources for other tasks. Something like that might be true for the internet too: it might be that insofar as iPhones take over the task of memory and time management, some brain-based capacities will atrophy [weaken] and the neural real estate will be repurposed.

Neil Levy, "Your Brain on the Internet: A Response to Susan Greenfield," The Conversation, August 7, 2012. http://theconversation.com.

brain changes associated with digital devices as undesirable, these changes may in fact represent positive new ways in which people can learn and remember things.

Learning and Memory

One factor that has spurred new ways of learning and remembering information is the overwhelming amount of information available on the Internet. People who wish to find out about any topic can do a Google search for certain keywords and will often be bombarded with hundreds of thousands of possible resources.

Psychology professor Betsy Sparrow of Columbia University has done extensive research on how the human brain has adapted to all this information. She calls these brain changes the Google Effect. Sparrow's research indicates that when people learn to rely on Google for information they want, they do not remember the information as well as they remember details from non-Internet sources. Instead, they remember where to find the information on the Internet. Sparrow likens this phenomenon to "using the Internet as a specialized external memory" and notes that "our brains rely on the Internet for memory in much the same way they rely on the memory of a friend, family member or co-worker. We remember less through knowing information itself than by knowing *where* the information can be found."[54]

Sparrow's research also indicates that people are more likely to remember information they believe is not available online. Thus, she believes that modern technologies are not making people less smart but are promoting different ways of learning. She suggests that understanding how people learn in the Internet age can possibly lead to new teaching methods that focus more on helping students understand, rather than memorize, facts and ideas.

Digital Devices and Brain Development

In addition to changing how people learn, research indicates that digital devices can affect brain development in babies and children. In the late 1990s and early 2000s many educators advocated introducing babies and toddlers to educational software that taught them to press computer keys and helped them learn about colors,

The search engine Google may be changing how people learn. At least one researcher suggests that people today may rely more on knowing where to find facts on the Internet than on committing facts to memory.

shapes, letters, and other concepts. At the same time, educational television programs like *Sesame Street* were also popular.

However, educators, psychologists, and pediatricians have changed their views about the benefits of screen technologies as more than fifty studies have found that the brains of young children develop better when they play actively and interact with humans. Based on this research, the American Academy of Pediatrics (AAP) recommends that children under age two should not spend any time watching television or using electronic media. The AAP also states that parents should limit screen time for older children to less than two hours per day. The AAP notes, "A child's brain develops rapidly during these first years, and young children learn best by interacting with people, not screens."[55]

Numerous studies indicate that electronic media exposure in young children is associated with slow language development and later problems with concentration. Pediatrician Dimitri Christakis of the University of Washington writes in a report on screen viewing that these findings are consistent with research showing that many of the connections in a child's brain develop in response to sensory stimulation—sights, smells, sounds, and touch—around them. Looking at a screen does not actively engage a child in these sensory experiences, so many connections do not develop. However, Christakis's research has led him to dispute the AAP recommendations against allowing babies under age two to use any digital devices. He notes that passively watching television does not enhance brain development, but playing interactive iPad games does help babies develop attention and language skills.

Neuroscientist Gary Small is one expert with concerns that excessive use of digital devices is negatively impacting brain development in older children as well as babies. Small writes that the combination of digital rather than face-to-face interactions and the constant stream of unpleasant videos and news articles on the Internet has resulted in what he calls digital natives—people born into the world of cell phones and the Internet—"desensitizing their neural circuits to the horrors they see, while not getting much, if any, off-line training in empathetic skills." When this happens, neural connections that control understanding other people (empathy) do not develop. Small believes this is worrisome because "when our brains become wired to disassociate from unpleasant experiences, we lose a part of what defines our humanity."[56]

Not all experts agree that the brain changes associated with digital use are leading to a lack of empathy. Amanda Lenhart of the Pew Internet & American Life Research Project believes that Small's research in no way proves that technology use is impairing empathy in most people. As Lenhart notes, "Teenagers told Pew researchers that they'd rather be with their friends in person than talking with them over electronic devices."[57] Likewise, many of the teens surveyed were sensitive to the fact that being with people provides different social cues than electronic communications do.

Impatience and Concentration

People accustomed to lightning-fast communications and Internet connections sometimes demonstrate impatience and an inability

"When our brains become wired to disassociate from unpleasant experiences, we lose a part of what defines our humanity."[56]

— UCLA neuroscientist Gary Small.

Two little boys entertain themselves with an iPad. At least one researcher believes that interactive iPad games can help babies develop attention and language skills.

to concentrate on lengthy tasks. These characteristics might illustrate another way in which brain development is being affected by digital technologies. A 2010 *New York Times* article reveals that educators are very concerned about the inability or unwillingness of many of their students to engage in tasks that require lengthy concentration or analytical thought. The article highlights a seventeen-year-old student named Vishal Singh who admits that his use of digital technologies contributed to his refusal to complete a summer homework project to read one book. Singh states that on You Tube "you can get a whole story in six minutes. A book takes so long. I prefer the immediate gratification."[58]

Studies also indicate that the trend of reading books and other documents on a screen is affecting learning and the capacity for deep thinking. As Watson points out in *Future Minds*, "Reading on a computer screen is fast and is suited to foraging for facts. In contrast, reading on paper is reflective and is better suited to trying to understand an overall argument or concept."[59] Researchers believe that concentrating on material on a screen is difficult for several reasons. For one thing, distractions like links and popups do not make it easy to fully concentrate. Studies show that the need to scroll on a computer is also distracting since the reader must split his concentration between scrolling and understanding the text. Turning pages on a paper book, on the other hand, does not require attention. Numerous studies show that people comprehend and remember material they read in paper books better than in books they read on a computer screen. For example, a 2013 study at the University of Stavanger in Norway found that students who read a story on paper scored better on a comprehension test than those who read the same story on a computer.

In response to people's growing impatience and inability to concentrate, educators and publishers of magazines and some books have started presenting information in short, easily digested chunks. This allows people to quickly read through material but does not allow them to learn about any topic in-depth.

Multitasking Minuses

Another trend experts believe is affecting people's ability to concentrate and learn is the digital multitasking in which many engage. A Kaiser Family Foundation report states that wireless digital devices have made multitasking easier and have exacerbated the multitasking trend. One seventeen-year-old boy who participated in a survey commented, "I multitask every second I am online. At this very moment I am watching TV, checking my email every two minutes, reading a newsgroup about who shot JFK, burning some music to a CD and writing this message."[60]

Studies show that even when people do not simultaneously play video games, text, watch television, and so on, just being online is a form of multitasking because of all the links, popups, and other distractions. As physician Carol J. Scott explains, "This endless barrage of data interrupts our train of thought and impacts our ability to focus. Over time, this constant onslaught of Facebook updates, Twitter alerts and other low-value information robs us of our ability to devote time to more attentive types of thinking."[61]

According to Harvard Medical School associate professor Michael Rich, the constant switching from one task to another is overwhelming people's brains with neuronal activity and leading to extensive brain rewiring. Rich believes this is mostly occurring

Multitasking and Driving

David L. Strayer of the University of Utah's research on cell phone use while driving indicates that the risks for drivers talking on a cell phone are as great as those for intoxicated drivers. Both react more slowly than normal to events on the road, and drivers talking on cell phones cause even more accidents than drunk drivers do. Strayer concludes that the impairments in cell phone drivers results from the distractions and attention lapses caused by trying to multitask. He also notes that "the driving impairments associated with handheld and hands-free cell phone conversations were not significantly different."

These findings call into question some state laws that prohibit talking on a handheld cell phone while driving but allow talking when using a hands-free device. Forty-four US states ban texting while driving, and some prohibit teens or new drivers from using a cell phone while driving. But although some advocates have proposed banning all cell phone use while driving, this has not happened in the United States. Given that more than 330 people were killed and 387,000 were injured in crashes involving distracted drivers in 2011, US transportation secretary Ray LaHood states in a 2013 report that turning off one's phone while driving is the best course of action.

David L. Strayer et al., "A Comparison of the Cell Phone Driver and the Drunk Driver," *Human Factors*, vol. 48, no. 2, Summer 2006, p. 388.

because "their brains are being rewarded not for staying on task but for jumping to the next thing."[62]

UCLA psychologist Russell Poldrack's research indicates that people who multitask also use different parts of the brain than those who devote their full attention to learning one thing. When people devote their full attention to one thing, the hippocampus is mainly involved in processing, storing, and remembering the information. People who try to learn while distracted with multitasking show the most activity in the striatum area of the brain. The striatum is important in learning new skills but is not helpful in remembering learned information. Poldrack states in a news article that the major importance of his findings is that "our study indicates that multi-tasking changes the way people learn."[63]

Many multitaskers say that multitasking makes them more productive, but researchers find multitasking's effects on the brain lead to a 40 percent loss in productivity because none of the tasks are receiving the individual's full attention. As psychologist Gary Winch explains in a Fox News article, "When it comes to attention and productivity, our brains have a finite amount. It's like a pie chart, and whatever we're working on is going to take up the majority of that pie. There's not a lot left over for other things with the exception of automatic behaviors like walking or chewing gum."[64] Indeed, developmental molecular biologist John Medina writes in his book *Brain Rules* that the human brain can only concentrate fully on one thing at a time. People who multitask end up learning less and producing inferior products or reports because their attention is unfocused.

One of the most controversial issues surrounding multitasking is cell phone use while driving. Lawmakers and behavior experts agree that texting while driving is unsafe at any time. However, disagreements arise over whether talking on cell phones should be allowed with or without hands-free devices like Bluetooth connections. Researchers like Stanford University communications professor Clifford Nass state that even though research indicates talking on a cell phone while driving is distracting, convincing the public not to do this is not easy. Nass notes that many multitaskers believe they are good at it; he states in a National Public Radio interview, "The people who multitask most frequently think they're actually best at it, and in fact, they're the worst at it."[65] Like other questions related to the effects of digital devices on mental processes, debates on this issue are not likely to disappear anytime soon.

"Our study indicates that multi-tasking changes the way people learn."[63]

— UCLA psychologist Russell Poldrack.

Facts

- According to developmental molecular biologist John Medina, research shows that people who multitask take twice as long to finish a given project and make 50 percent more errors than those who concentrate on one project at a time.

- A Kaiser Family Foundation study found that 50 percent of American students ages eight to eighteen use the Internet, watch television, text, and use other digital devices while doing homework, even though these distractions impair their concentration.

- The same Kaiser Family Foundation study reports that children ages eight to eighteen spend an average of seven hours and thirty-eight minutes per day with various digital media.

- Despite warnings by the American Pediatric Society about the undesirable effects of digital media on babies' brain development, 55 percent of American parents revealed in a 2013 Center on Media and Human Development survey that they are not concerned about media use by their small children.

- A 2013 study by the US Department of Transportation found that 660,000 people are using cell phones or manipulating other electronic devices while driving at any given moment, despite laws prohibiting distracted driving and extensive publicity about the risks.

How Do Digital Devices Affect Physical and Mental Health?

Although many experts believe that digital devices have caused or contributed to a variety of physical and mental health problems, others argue that these devices have merely led to behavior changes that should not be considered diseases or disorders. Some mental health experts who hold digital technologies responsible for various mental disorders think these disorders may result from the brain changes these technologies cause. Others believe genetic or personality factors, rather than specific technologies, are mostly responsible for increases in certain health problems and conditions.

Fitness and Obesity

A 2013 study by researchers at Northwestern University found that 61 percent of American parents are concerned that their children's physical fitness suffers when they spend a lot of time on digital devices. This concern stems from research such as a 2011 study that found that children who are allowed to use digital devices in their bedrooms have a 30 percent increase in their risk of obesity and increased risks of type 2 diabetes and heart disease. Indeed, the AAP advises parents to limit their children's screen time because time spent on sedentary activities leaves less time for active playing and sports that build muscles and heart health.

While evidence supports the notion that decreasing sedentary activities and increasing physical activities is important, controversies exist about whether all sedentary activities contribute equally to obesity and obesity-related problems. Some studies show that watching television, reading, and using computers all raise the risks of obesity. But other studies indicate that specific sedentary activities are most strongly linked to obesity. Such studies have led some experts to suggest that bans on specific types of technology use, rather than on overall use, are prudent. For example, a 2010 study published in the *American Journal of Public Health* found that watching television ads for sugary, fatty foods led to children eating nearly twice as many snacks as children who watched television with no food advertisements. The researchers concluded, "The evidence does not support the contention that television viewing contributes to obesity because it is a sedentary activity. Television advertising, rather than viewing per se, is associated with obesity."[66]

Other studies challenge the widely held view that increases in access to mobile digital devices have led to decreases in time spent on physical activity. According to a 2010 Kaiser Family Foundation report, "Contrary to the public perception that media use displaces physical activity, those young people who are the heaviest media users report spending similar amounts of time exercising or being physically active as other young people their age who are not heavy media users."[67]

Some psychologists have suggested that heavy media use contributes to exercise because seeing slim, toned people who are considered to be attractive on social media, as well as in television shows and movies, may motivate people to strive to become slim and attractive. Others believe that digital devices have contributed to recent increases in eating disorders such as anorexia and bulimia. For example, psychologist Larry Rosen writes in his book *iDisorder* that while thin models and actors on television, movies, and print magazines used to primarily fuel eating disorders, the Internet and digital devices "burst onto the scene, presenting beauty images 24/7 on all of our devices, and this is undoubtedly exacerbating this problem."[68]

Young people who are active in sports build muscles and heart health. Those who spend hours with their digital devices rather than engaging in physical activity are at greater risk of becoming overweight and developing conditions such as Type 2 diabetes and heart disease.

Numerous studies support this contention and have found that websites that openly promote anorexia have contributed to these increases. At the same time, mental health experts have pointed out that strengthening the presence and outreach of sites that seek to help, rather than encourage, these types of damaging behaviors, can potentially offset the effects of media that fuel eating disorders.

Controversies over Narcissism

Similar debates have emerged over whether digital devices are responsible for increasing the risk of or actually triggering certain mental disorders. Rosen's research shows that many people who constantly text, send e-mails, and post photos and status updates have symptoms of a psychiatric disorder called narcissistic personality disorder—believing the world revolves around them and that everything they do is important. In a 2011 study Rosen found that people of all ages who used digital devices the most were the most narcissistic.

Other experts caution against blaming reported increases in narcissism entirely on digital technologies. Psychologists Twenge and Campbell write in their book *The Narcissism Epidemic* that permissive parenting and the practice of discouraging excellence and competition in school are in fact mostly responsible for increases in narcissism: "Few boundaries are set by families, and teachers tell children they are 'stars' and 'winners' even as performance stays stagnant."[69] The philosophy behind unconditional praise is that it enhances a child's self-esteem. However, studies show that parents who do not set boundaries for their children and who praise everything they do teach them that they can do whatever they want, whenever they want.

Twenge and Campbell also believe certain aspects of modern technologies worsen the narcissistic tendencies wrought by this type of parenting. They explain that the Internet is "a conduit for individual narcissism. . . . It allows people to present an inflated and self-focused view of themselves to the world, and encourages them to spend hours each day contemplating their images."[70]

Other researchers, however, challenge beliefs that the incidence of narcissism has risen at all. Some question the reliability of the questionnaires and other methods used to assess whether people are narcissistic. Psychologists Trzesniewski and Donnellan also believe older people tend to judge younger ones whose behaviors are new and different as being selfish or uncaring because they do not understand these behaviors. Indeed, Trzesniewski reports that her research indicates that children and teens today "are just as narcissistic as we were at their age."[71] Technology might simply make narcissistic behavior more visible.

Digital Devices and ADHD

Controversies also exist about whether digital devices increase the risk of or worsen existing cases of ADHD. Experts have observed

Multitasking Stress

Research indicates that multitasking and the constant need to stay on top of e-mails, texts, and other digital communications is extremely stressful and can lead to a variety of health problems. A 2012 study by researchers at the University of California, Irvine (UCI), showed that multitaskers had consistently higher heart rates than nonmultitaskers. Multitaskers also stated that they always felt stressed from being in a constant state of "high alert." Long-term stress from multitasking day after day leads to abnormally high levels of stress hormones, such as cortisol, which elevates heart rate and blood pressure, impairs the immune system, leads to digestive problems and weight gain, and impairs sleep.

During the UCI study, one group of office workers took an "email vacation" for five days. They did their regular work, but did not receive or send e-mails. Lead researcher Gloria Mark explains, "We found that when you remove email from workers' lives, they multitask less and experience less stress." The workers stated that having no e-mail made them feel much more relaxed and better able to concentrate and do their jobs well.

Quoted in UC Irvine Today, "Email 'Vacations' Decrease Stress, Increase Concentration," May 3, 2012. http://today.uci.edu.

that some children with the disorder have trouble sitting still and concentrating in school but can sit and play video games for hours at home. Scientists believe this is because video games provide constant, fast-paced, changing activity that causes the brain to release large amounts of the neurotransmitter dopamine. Neurotransmitters are brain chemicals that transmit signals between neurons. One of dopamine's functions is to make people feel good when it acts on the so-called reward centers in the brain.

Some neuroscientists believe that when children with ADHD become accustomed to constantly feeling good from dopamine release, their brains crave more and more stimulation from fast-paced activities. Paying attention in slow-paced environments like school becomes more and more difficult for them, resulting in behaviors that indicate worsening ADHD. These experts thus believe that video games worsen existing ADHD or provoke it in genetically vulnerable children. Other research suggests that similar brain mechanisms may be involved in people who are addicted to computer games or to drugs. A 2010 study by Israeli scientist Aviv Weinstein found that people with computer game addictions and drug addictions have fewer than normal dopamine receptors (neural structures that take up dopamine) in the area of the brain that plays a role in feelings of pleasure and reward. Weinstein believes this supports the idea that people prone to addictive behaviors and to ADHD need more intense and frequent dopamine release to experience positive feelings.

Other experts believe digital technologies like television and video games are contributing to increases in ADHD because early exposure to these devices prevents the brain from developing normal neural connections in areas that govern attention. Studies by Christakis of the University of Washington indicate that children ages one to three who watch two to three hours of television per day have a 30 percent increased risk of developing ADHD by age seven. Each additional hour increases the risk by 10 percent. Christakis notes that this increased risk comes from more television time depriving young children of the real-life experiences that help normal neural connections form.

Studies by psychologist Edward Swing and his associates show that a lack of neural connections may also underlie research findings that children who play the most video games have the greatest risk of attention problems. This research controlled for factors that could indicate that children who are prone to attention problems tend to play more video games. However, the researchers write that their studies still do not prove that playing video games prevents normal neural connections from forming or causes attention problems since other, unknown factors may be responsible.

Digital Depression

As with ADHD, the incidence of depression has skyrocketed in recent years, and some researchers believe digital devices and social media may increase the risk or even cause depression in vulnerable people. Numerous instances where social media postings and online bullying have led adolescents to commit suicide have led some psychologists to conclude that teens are especially vulnerable to being pushed into depression from digital technologies. Indeed, a 2010 study found that teens who use the Internet excessively are 2.5 times more likely to suffer from depression than other teens. However, experts state that individuals who commit suicide were probably already depressed, meaning social media did not actually cause their depression. In a *Huffington Post* article Lidia Bernik of the National Suicide Prevention Lifeline also points out that although online bullying can provoke depression and suicide, it is usually only one of many contributing factors. Often, people blame online bullying because "it's almost easier to understand—someone was victimized, and then they killed themselves."[72]

Although no one has proved that any sort of technology causes depression, many people thought researchers had established a causal connection after psychologist Joanne Davila published a 2011 study in which she referred to "Facebook depression."[73] Davila used the term to describe preteens and teens who spend a lot of time on Facebook and then develop classic symptoms of depression. Davila later claimed she never stated that Facebook causes depression, but she was widely criticized for implying a causal connection and for stating that Facebook depression exists. Technology journalist Larry Magid, for example, wrote in a *Huffington Post* article that "it's a made-up condition which, despite claims to the contrary, is not backed up by any research. . . . Of course, people can become depressed when they encounter depressing content on Facebook, but that would be true in any venue. Why not create conditions like school depression, playground depression or home depression?"[74]

"Our research indicates that excessive Internet use is associated with depression, but what we don't know is which comes first— are depressed people drawn to the Internet or does the Internet cause depression?"[75]

— Leeds University research psychologist Catriona Morrison.

Other studies have found links between various digital media and depression, but again, none has proved causality. In one landmark 2010 study, research psychologist Catriona Morrison found that Internet addicts are significantly more depressed than nonaddicts. Morrison stated in a BBC News article, "Our research indicates that excessive Internet use is associated with depression, but what we don't know is which comes first—are depressed people drawn to the Internet or does the Internet cause depression?"[75] Some critics question the importance of Morrison's findings, stating that depression can be equally linked to many other pastimes. For instance, psychiatrist Vaughan Bell of King's College London

Digital devices and social media, which are so much a part of modern life, may increase the risk of depression—especially in teenagers. However, most experts caution that chronic depression has many causes.

contends, "There are genuinely people who are depressed or anxious who use the internet to the exclusion of the rest of their lives, but there are similar people who watch too much TV, bury themselves in books, or go shopping to excess."[76]

New Disorders

Although experts believe most efforts to classify new types of so-called technology diseases are misguided, substantial evidence shows that modern digital devices have indeed led to some genuinely new disorders. For example, psychologist Rosen's contention that behaviors such as compulsively checking one's smartphone for updates, being unable to concentrate on prolonged tasks, and compulsively multitasking represent a new disease is widely accepted by psychologists. Rosen acknowledges that although these behaviors share characteristics of traditional mental disorders such as attention deficit disorder and obsessive-compulsive disorder, "what we are looking at is a new disorder, one that combines elements of many psychiatric maladies and is centered on the way we all relate to technology and media: an iDisorder."[77]

Rosen's book *iDisorder* discusses many manifestations of iDisorders, and other mental health experts also have coined new terms to describe new technology-related disorders. For instance, psychologist Jim Taylor of the University of San Francisco has written extensively about disconnectivity anxiety (DA)—the label he gives to the worry and unease that result when people who feel compelled to constantly communicate with their digital devices are deprived of this ability. In one extreme case of DA, a man was so upset when his wife and children insisted that he disconnect from his cell phone and laptop on a family vacation that he drove everyone home and canceled the vacation.

Another Internet-related condition that has received a great deal of attention is cyberchondria—a modern derivative of hypochondria. Hypochondriacs are individuals who imagine or fake having certain diseases, even after doctors assure them there is nothing wrong. Cyberchondriacs become anxious about their health and often self-diagnose themselves after accessing health-related information online.

"Every person is about four websites away from deciding they have cancer and are going to die. There is just so much bad information on the Internet."[78]

— Northwestern Memorial Hospital emergency room physician Rahul Khare.

Many doctors believe the ability to access millions of health-related websites is a good thing, as long as people only consult reliable sites and do not try to diagnose themselves. But 35 percent of American adults say they go online to try to self-diagnose based on their symptoms, and they often consult unreliable websites. As Northwestern Memorial Hospital emergency room physician Rahul Khare states in a *Prevention* article, "Every person is about four websites away from deciding they have cancer and are going to die. There is just so much bad information on the Internet."[78] Indeed, a Nottingham University study found that only 39 percent of the first one hundred websites listed on Google in response to queries about certain symptoms offer correct information. To avoid this bad information, doctors recommend that people consult only legitimate websites such as those from the National Institutes of Health or CDC. In addition, well-known universities and clinics like the Cleveland Clinic provide reliable information.

The consequences of cyberchondria can range from harmless to serious unless a legitimate doctor is consulted. In one case, a woman became convinced that her infant was autistic after she read on an unreliable website that babies who do not smile or laugh as much as most babies probably have autism. She was ready to begin treatment, but luckily consulted a pediatrician first. The pediatrician informed her that it is impossible to diagnose autism in infants and that any therapy would not be started until age two if her child was actually diagnosed with autism. In other cases people started taking over-the-counter medications or changed their diet after self-diagnosing and finding online treatment advice. Their true medical problems were not diagnosed and became increasingly worse because they failed to consult a doctor.

Technology Addictions

Although many doctors now use the term *cyberchondriac*, controversy surrounds the use of terms for technology-related addictions. Some experts believe digital devices have led to new types of ad-

Faking Disease and the Internet

A cyberchondriac is a new type of hypochondriac who imagines or fakes illness based on online information. The same profusion of online medical information that produces cyberchondriacs has also led to people using the Internet to con others into donating money to help fight a faked illness. In 2012, for example, a judge sent twenty-seven-year-old Jamie Toler of Arizona to jail after she set up a donation website that raised more than $8,000 for her supposed breast cancer treatments. She used the money to pay for breast augmentation surgery. Also in 2012, Texas high school student Angie Gomez was jailed after defrauding classmates and others of $17,000 through a fake charity website she set up to help her fight leukemia she did not have.

Psychiatrist Marc Feldman terms a similar modern trend *Munchausen by Internet*. Traditional Munchausen syndrome is a mental illness that involves faking illness to gain attention from doctors. Munchausen by Internet involves using online support groups for this purpose. For instance, thirty-seven-year-old Mandy Wilson of Australia wove an elaborate tale about having leukemia to gain sympathy from women on the Connected Moms website. Three years later another woman discovered the truth. Feldman believes incidents of cyberchondria and Internet conning are increasing because it is so easy to obtain disease information, join online support groups, and launch crowd-funding pleas.

dictions, including Internet, cell phone, and video game addictions. Others believe that those who overuse digital technologies are not actually addicts. Mental health experts define behaviors or habits as addictions if the behavior disrupts other aspects of the individual's life, the individual feels anxious if deprived of the

A young woman in Tokyo checks her phone for messages while waiting for a train. Studies from Japan show that 30 percent of eighth grade students suffer from "text-message dependency."

relevant substance or behavior, and the individual needs increasing amounts of the substance or behavior to feel satisfied. Psychologists use a variety of questionnaires to determine whether an individual suffers from a technology-related addiction. For instance, the Cell-Phone Overuse Scale and the Chen Internet Addiction Scale are two recently developed assessment tools.

However, although many experts talk about Internet addictions and thousands of people worldwide admit they have them, these addictions are not recognized psychiatric disorders in the United States. China was the first country to classify Internet addiction as a clinical disorder in 2008. The Chinese definition of *Internet addiction* includes people who spend more than six hours per day online, experience compulsions to be online, and/or become anxious if deprived of Internet use.

Various Internet addictions are especially prevalent throughout Asia, and hundreds of treatment clinics have been opened to help affected people. In Japan, for instance, studies reveal that 30 percent of eighth-graders suffer from so-called text-message dependency. These teens constantly check messages on their phones, even during the night, and admit that cell phone use interferes with their daily lives.

Overuse Versus Addiction

Many American experts believe the incidence of Internet addictions in this country warrants its classification as a mental illness as well. Indeed, a Stanford University study found that one in eight Americans behaves as if he or she has an Internet addiction. Other experts, however, question whether the constant use of digital technologies qualifies as addictive behavior. Some view these behaviors as just a part of everyday modern life for many people, especially young people. Western Washington University psychology professor Ira Hyman, for example, writes in *Psychology Today,*

> I think we are seeing an emerging form of social interaction. Teens and young adults are natives in the land of technology. . . . Their social lives are tied up in these machines; they live across the internet and airways. . . . Staying constantly in touch with your entire circle of friends may be the new norm in tech-land. . . . If being constantly in touch through your cell phone is normal, then it probably isn't an addiction.[79]

Thus, experts like Hyman believe the 73 percent of Americans who say they would feel panicked if they lost their cell phone are simply accustomed to life in the twenty-first century.

Other psychologists argue that studies showing brain changes in so-called Internet or video game addicts are evidence that these compulsions are true addictions. Several studies show that when people find certain online activities pleasurable, their brains are rewired to expect and need the dopamine release that goes along with stimulating the brain's reward centers. Similar rewiring occurs in the brains of drug addicts. In addition,

"If being constantly in touch through your cell phone is normal, then it probably isn't an addiction."[79]

— Western Washington University psychology professor Ira Hyman.

Rosen writes in *iDisorder* that "researchers have noted that the consequences of technology addiction are similar to the consequences of chemical addictions such as drugs or alcohol and can include financial problems, job loss, and relationship breakdowns."[80]

Boston College psychologist Peter Gray, however, disputes the contention that people should be called addicts just because their brain pleasure centers are active and they crave their digital devices. Gray writes in *Psychology Today*, "If we were to define every activity that activates the brain's 'Pleasure centers' as addictive, and therefore to be curtailed, we would have to curtail everything that's fun." Instead of calling everyone who spends a lot of time doing something an addict, Gray suggests, "let's just call it a time management problem and figure out constructive ways to deal with it."[81]

Controversies over whether Internet and related overuse are truly addictions are likely to continue. Some commentators have suggested that many people are using the term *addiction* to excuse irresponsible behaviors like neglecting one's family while playing nonstop video games or to justify rude behavior. For example, after actor Alec Baldwin was kicked off an American Airlines flight in 2011 for refusing to turn off his cell phone, he claimed his addiction to the game *Words with Friends* led to his uncooperative behavior. A commentator for the *Washington Post* remarked, "Well another shocker, an entitled, whiny Hollywood prima donna acting like the rules don't apply to them."[82] With continued research into the brain's functions, perhaps experts will be able to confirm whether technology addictions are true diseases.

"Researchers have noted that the consequences of technology addiction are similar to the consequences of chemical addictions such as drugs or alcohol and can include financial problems, job loss, and relationship breakdowns."[80]

— California State University, Dominguez Hills, research psychologist Larry Rosen.

Facts

- The Pew Research Center reports that 80 percent of Internet users have looked up health-related information online.

- The CDC reports that the incidence of ADHD increased 30 percent between the late 1990s and 2010. Many experts believe overuse of digital devices has contributed to these increases.

- Because of her belief that people born and raised with modern digital devices are more narcissistic than those in previous generations, psychologist Jean Twenge has labeled those born during and after the 1980s *Generation Me*.

- Studies find that over half of American teenagers report checking their cell phones all the time, 30 percent check their social networks all the time, and 75 percent check text messages at least once every hour.

- An MTV poll found that 58 percent of young people worry about missing out on something if they disconnect from their phones. Sixty-six percent find this need to always be connected exhausting.

- A 2012 *Time* magazine poll found that 75 percent of people ages twenty-five to twenty-nine sleep with their cell phones.

CHAPTER FIVE

Do Digital Devices Promote Crime?

D igital technologies have led to new types of crimes that were not possible before the Internet and mobile devices existed. Debates have emerged, however, about whether these devices promote crime or have just given criminals new and easier ways of doing what they do. Marist College computer scientist Jan L. Harrington, for example, writes in her book *Technology and Society*, "The Internet has made it easier to commit a number of crimes, although if we look carefully, none of the crimes is really new. . . . An information thief no longer has to visit the offices where the information he wants is stored; the theft can be done remotely over a computer network."[83] But other experts believe some digital technologies, such as violent video games and social media, drive otherwise nonviolent people to do violent things. Other controversies have arisen about whether technology-related activities such as cyberbullying should be considered crimes or expressions of free speech.

The New World of Cybercrimes

Among the cybercrimes that have emerged from digital devices are hacking (unauthorized break-ins on computers, databases, and mobile digital devices), malware (computer viruses, worms, and other bugs that can disable computers or steal personal data), and phishing (trying to con people into giving up personal or financial data). In addition, criminals establish websites and use untraceable cell phones to sell stolen credit card numbers and to communicate with like-minded individuals to plan terror attacks and similar events. Criminals also hide behind aliases on social networking sites and chatrooms, where they victimize unsuspecting children, teens, and adults.

Dealing with the vast array of computer-related crimes is now a priority for law enforcement agencies. According to an article in *Security Management* magazine, "Fighting cybercrime is now the FBI's third-largest priority, after terrorism and espionage. . . . The FBI currently has full-time cybercrime agents working in about 60 countries."[84] The Secret Service and the FBI are the main US agencies that investigate cybercrimes. Both work with numerous law enforcement agencies around the world to combat a growing number of cybercriminals.

Tracking and arresting cybercriminals is not easy. For example, it took FBI supervisory agent J. Keith Mularski two years of undercover work to find the major operators of an online credit card theft and document forging company called DarkMarket. These criminals hid behind aliases and false Internet servers in several countries to evade detection. Mularski carefully cultivated his undercover identity of "Master Splyntr" to become a trusted member of the operation. He finally tracked down the true identities of nearly sixty DarkMarket leaders. One of these criminals, Cagatay Evyapan of Turkey, kidnapped and tortured another DarkMarket member he suspected of betraying the group before he (Evyapan) was arrested. Evyapan was known for aggressively marketing high-quality ATM card skimmers and other devices that allowed thieves to steal customers' account numbers and passwords.

Hacking and Online Theft

Cybercriminals all over the world also use the Internet to hack into computers and databases containing sensitive information about individuals, businesses, and organizations. Many plant spyware and other malware by enticing people to click on e-mails and websites that appear to be from legitimate companies. They then gain access to personal passwords for bank accounts, health data, and

A group of hackers from eastern Europe stole 40 million credit card numbers and 70 million customer addresses and phone numbers from Target's databases in 2013. Digital technology makes cybercrimes of this scale possible.

many other types of online records to steal identities and money.

The number of people affected by these crimes is staggering. In 2013, for example, a group of eastern European hackers stole 40 million credit card numbers and 70 million customer addresses and phone numbers from Target's databases. In August 2014 the *New York Times* revealed that a Russian crime ring stole 1.2 billion Internet user names and passwords from more than four hundred thousand websites, including social media sites and e-mail providers. The hackers used software that trolled the Internet for security vulnerabilities on millions of websites.

In other types of hacking cases, hackers exploit security defects in computer operating systems or Internet service provider networks. For example, in April 2014 hackers exploited a simple programming error to breach millions of smartphones and tablets, along with major websites such as Yahoo!, the University of Michigan, and the Canadian government's Revenue Agency. The

Canadian government announced that these hackers stole about nine hundred social security numbers from their databases. The defect, known as the Heartbleed bug, affected devices that ran on the Android 4.1.1 operating system and that used a type of encryption called OpenSSL. Encryption software scrambles data so it is incomprehensible to anyone who does not have a digital key to unlock the information.

OpenSSL encryption provides security for many online applications, including e-mail, instant messaging, and user names and passwords on secure sites. When the Heartbleed bug was discovered, technology companies estimated that 66 percent of all Internet users used OpenSSL. The bug gave hackers easy access to the digital keys that unlocked communications and personal data on any website using this system. The only way to stop this access was to install a patch, or software fix, released by the software manufacturer.

Insider Hacking

Sometimes hacking involves insiders at a particular institution. For example, in 2013 Cedars-Sinai Hospital in Los Angeles fired six workers for illegally accessing the electronic hospital records of fourteen patients. Most were interested in looking at actress Kim Kardashian's records after she gave birth to her daughter, North West. Federal laws known as the Health Insurance Portability and Accountability Act (HIPAA) prohibit unauthorized people from accessing patient records, but many hospital and health care workers violate these laws out of curiosity, to sell information to tabloid newspapers, or to steal financial information or patient identities. In one of the largest such breaches, UCLA Hospital office worker Lawanda Jackson illegally accessed 939 patient records between 2004 and 2007 using her supervisor's password. Jackson sold information on celebrities such as pop star Britney Spears and actress Farrah Fawcett to the *National Enquirer* for thousands of dollars. Jackson would have received jail time and up to $250,000 in fines, but she died of cancer before the courts could impose her sentence.

Millions of private health records have been breached by insiders or other types of hackers despite strict laws mandating employee training that emphasizes the serious consequences of such breaches. These breaches have led to controversies about whether digital technologies and electronic medical records are turning formerly moral employees into criminals or whether the ease of breaching electronic files and tracking employees' digital footprints have simply heightened awareness of an ongoing problem.

Most legal and behavior experts believe insider breaches result from a combination of easy access to electronic files and morally weak individuals. As health care journalist Anne Polta, who writes for the *West Central Tribune* in Minnesota, explains,

A hospital employee in Los Angeles illegally accessed patient records of celebrities such as pop star Britney Spears (pictured). The employee then sold some of this information to a tabloid newspaper.

For all the resources that have been poured into HIPAA compliance—passwords, data encryption, secure servers, staff training and the like—many data breaches seem to be less about technology and more about basic human nature: in other words, the urge to snoop and the lapses in judgment that lead health care workers into this less-than-ethical behavior. . . . Although no one likes to acknowledge it, snooping has probably taken place in health care for a very long time. These days, though, the temptations seem to be greater and electronic medical records have made it easier to indulge one's curiosity.[85]

Threats to Society

Along with cybercrimes such as hacking affecting individuals, businesses, and institutions, many experts are concerned that the misuse of digital technologies offers criminals unprecedented opportunities to threaten society as a whole. Preet Bharara, the US attorney for the Southern District of New York, commented in a 2012 *New York Times* opinion piece that cybercrime threatens the very existence of America: "Some cybercrime is aimed directly at our national security, imperiling our infrastructure, government secrets and public safety. . . . As the United States attorney in Manhattan, I have come to worry about few things as much as the gathering cyberthreat."[86] Bharara asserted that law enforcement agencies and businesses are not doing enough to prevent many types of cybercrimes, such as those where hackers break into military databases, and he encouraged more widespread risk assessments and measures to protect important data.

On the other hand, law enforcement and computer security specialists point out that keeping up with cybercrime is a struggle. As online security expert Steve Bennett writes, as soon as new methods of blocking and fighting cybercrime are developed, "cybercriminals continue to discover new vulnerabilities, and attacks are becoming more sophisticated, widespread, and easier to execute."[87]

"Cybercriminals continue to discover new vulnerabilities, and attacks are becoming more sophisticated, widespread, and easier to execute."[87]

— Online security specialist Steve Bennett.

Murder by Hacking

Technology experts are concerned about a new type of digital-device crime called medical cybercrime. Although no one has been caught committing this type of crime, hackers could easily use smartphones to remotely steal people's wireless medical device security codes and instruct the device to do something that kills the person. In 2011 computer security expert and insulin pump user Jay Radcliffe demonstrated how hackers could breach his pump's security features and program the pump to deliver a lethal dose of insulin. Many diabetics use electronic insulin pumps to administer their daily insulin shots. Radcliffe said his intent was to alert pump manufacturers so they would improve security features. However, he received numerous angry e-mails stating that he had given hackers the knowledge they needed to kill people with diabetes.

With more and more wireless medical devices out there, law enforcement agencies believe the threat of medical cybercrime is real. A 2012 episode of the TV show *Homeland* highlighted the issue when terrorists assassinated the US vice president by hacking his heart pacemaker and instructing it to deliver huge electric shocks that caused a fatal heart attack. Computer security experts confirmed this could really happen and leave no traces of tampering.

An event in April 2007 vividly illustrates how vulnerable societies are to being devastated by electronic disruptions. The government and national economy in Estonia shut down after unknown computer users flooded government, banking, and communications websites with huge amounts of cybertraffic. This occurred after the Estonian government upset its Russian citizens and Russians outside Estonia by relocating a statue honoring Russian soldiers killed during World War II. The cyberattacks came from outside Estonia, and Estonian government officials believe the Russian government or nationalistic groups encouraged millions of Russians to keep visiting the Estonian sites so the cybertraffic would force them to shut down. This is exactly what happened, though no one ever proved who was responsible for the traffic. Estonia had to cut all its Internet ties to stop the effects from spreading. This prevented most institutions in the country from operating. The cyberattacks stopped after a couple of weeks, but the Estonian government considered them to be an invasion, just as though a physical army had attacked the country.

Cell Phone Bombs

In other threats to society, mobile devices have made crimes that threaten public safety easier to coordinate and carry out. Terrorists used to set off bombs remotely using timers, but cell phones have given them easier ways to achieve their goals. In fact, hundreds of American soldiers have been killed in Iraq and Afghanistan after terrorists have placed improvised explosive devices on roadways and have detonated them remotely using cell phones. Terrorists have used cell phone bombs in attacks on civilians as well. For example, on March 11, 2004, Muslim terrorists set off ten bombs on four trains in Madrid, Spain. The bombs killed nearly two hundred people and wounded about eighteen hundred others. The bombs were placed in backpacks and hooked up to cell phones. When terrorists called these phones from another phone, the ringing activated a switch that detonated the bombs.

In a more recent development, on July 6, 2014, the US Transportation Security Administration banned uncharged cell phones and laptops on flights to the United States originating from overseas locations. This measure was implemented because intelligence agencies determined that Muslim terrorists had developed bombs that resemble phone or computer batteries and can thus escape detection by security screening devices. Officials believe that devices that cannot be turned on may pose a threat because the battery may have been replaced by a bomb. News outlets reported that Apple iPhones and Samsung Galaxy phones in particular are being subjected to intense screening.

Bullying and Criminal Behavior

Although there is little debate about whether hacking and terrorist activities should be classified as crimes, heated controversies do exist about whether other types of digital-device misuse, such as cyberbullying, constitute crimes or free speech. These controversies center on numerous cases in which online bullying has led adolescents and young adults to kill themselves. Legal and moral disputes have arisen about whether people who bully others online or share private photos are criminally responsible for causing those they bully to commit suicide.

In one case, on September 10, 2013, twelve-year-old Rebecca Sedwick of Lakeland, Florida, killed herself by jumping off a cement silo at an abandoned cement factory after being repeatedly cyberbullied by classmates led by Katelyn Roman and Guadalupe Shaw. Police searched Sedwick's cell phone and found a barrage of hurtful messages on Kik Messenger, Instagram, Ask.fm, and other social media apps. In one post, Shaw wrote, "Drink bleach and die." She later wrote, "Yes ik (I know) I bullied REBECCA nd she killed her self but IDGAF (I don't give a f—k)."[88]

Based on these messages, police arrested Roman and Shaw and charged them with stalking and cyberbullying. Antibullying advocates applauded the charges as a positive step toward letting bullies know their behavior would have consequences. Debbie Johnston, whose son Jeffrey committed suicide after cyberbullying, told CNN, "We have finally reached a tipping point where adults are taking this seriously. . . . Law enforcement needs to enforce the laws that are on the books and stop turning a blind eye simply because these are children."[89]

However, Roman's and Shaw's attorneys argued that the girls had a First Amendment right to free speech. They also stated that Sedwick had mental issues such as depression that drove her to suicide. Attorney Richard Herman told CNN, "This young girl [Sedwick] had a history. She tried to kill herself before. We have First Amendment issues here. Is it really bullying?"[90]

A month after their arrest, prosecutors dropped the charges against Shaw and Roman due to a lack of evidence. A judge or-

A US military truck burns after hitting a roadside bomb in Iraq. Mobile devices have been used by terrorists to remotely set off bombs in Iraq and Afghanistan.

dered them to receive counseling, and they were suspended from school. A firestorm of public criticism erupted, with some commentators asserting that police were too quick to file charges and others calling for new laws to make punishing bullies easier. Many commentators blamed Sedwick's death on factors other than bullying. These factors included the school administrators who failed to stop the bullying, Shaw's and Roman's parents, and the social media sites that supposedly promote this type of behavior. Criticism against the cell phone messaging app Ask.fm, where some of the most offensive comments against Sedwick were posted, was especially widespread. Numerous advocates for shutting down Ask.fm reiterated the urgency of signing petitions to make this happen. This campaign began after sixteen teens around the world killed themselves after vicious bullying on Ask.fm between 2012 and 2013. Ask.fm changed some of its safety policies in response to these demands. However, many technology experts emphasize that since social media is here to stay, it is more important that parents teach their children how to use it correctly rather than faulting the technologies.

Online Disinhibition

While many people blame acts like cyberbullying on parents or digital technologies, research shows that this behavior mostly results from individuals losing their reluctance to display their true personality in the online world. Indeed, hiding behind digital communications tends to make people forget that others with whom they are interacting are real people and that online behavior can have real-life consequences. They are then more likely to say things they would not say face-to-face or to commit crimes against others. Experts call this the online disinhibition effect. Psychologist John Suler first described this phenomenon in an article in the journal *CyberPsychology and Behavior* in 2004. Since then, online disinhibition has been studied extensively. Psychologists have discovered that online disinhibition can have both positive and negative consequences. They call the positive effects *benign disinhibition* and the negative ones *toxic disinhibition*.

Benign disinhibition often occurs when people join online support or discussion groups to exchange information and mutual support with others in similar situations. Studies discussed in the book *Cyberbullying Through the New Media* reveal that "people who have never met share deep emotions that they would never share in the context of an offline relationship." In particular, "some adolescents may confess their difficulties in socializing with peers, their doubts about sexuality or sexual identity without fear of the consequences to themselves."[91]

Toxic disinhibition, in contrast, can lead bullies and others who might have restrained themselves offline to unleash angry, hurtful tirades against online targets. In such cases, studies indicate that modern technologies do not create bullies but merely give them a convenient way of ramping up their attacks while hid-

"In contrast to common belief, we now know that many people, when immersed in cyberspace, remove their offline masks and games and expose their more authentic selves."[92]

— University of Haifa psychology professor and researcher Azy Barak.

Bad Technology or Bad People?

In October 2010 twenty-two-year-old Alexandra Tobias of Jacksonville, Florida, shook her three-month-old son, Dylan, so violently that he died. Tobias claimed she was angry because Dylan's nonstop crying interrupted her *Farmville* game on Facebook. In May 2011 fifteen-year-old Kirsten Iovinelli of Tahuya, Washington, shot and wounded her father with a hunting bow after he took away her cell phone. She prevented him from calling for help, but he managed to crawl to his car and drive to a neighbor's house. In April 2014 twenty-two-year-old Vineet Singh of India shot and killed his online girl-friend, Jyoti Kori. The two met in person after communicating online for three years. Singh told police he was angry because Kori posted a photo of a film actress as her profile picture and claimed to be a twenty-one-year-old single woman. She was really a forty-five-year-old married mother of three.

Numerous similar incidents have led to debates about whether digital technologies, particularly addictions to these technologies, cause people to commit crimes they would not normally commit. Many mental health experts believe cyberaddictions change the brain and drive people to these crimes. Others believe these technologies are merely the catalyst that spurs violent acts in people with violent tendencies.

ing behind an online shield. As researcher Azy Barak explains in *Psychological Aspects of Cyberspace: Theory, Research, Applications*, "In contrast to common belief, we now know that many people, when immersed in cyberspace, remove their offline masks and games and expose their more authentic selves"[92] because of online disinhibition.

Media Exposure and Aggression

Similar controversies have emerged over whether playing violent video games turns mild-mannered people into violent criminals. On the one hand, numerous studies indicate a clear link between exposure to violent media and aggressive behavior. One study by psychologist Christopher Barlett found that college students who played *Mortal Kombat: Deadly Alliance* for fifteen minutes were more aggressive toward others than students who played a nonviolent game. A 2012 study by researchers at Brock University indicated that "greater violent video game play predicted higher levels of aggression over time"[93] in adolescents.

Other studies support the notion that watching violent television shows and/or playing violent video games teaches people that aggressive or criminal behavior is an acceptable method of dealing with frustration or anger. University of Michigan psychology professor L. Rowell Huesmann believes this is partly because frequent exposure to violent media desensitizes children and others to violence. "When you're exposed to violence day in and day out, it loses its emotional impact on you. Once you're emotionally numb to violence, it's much easier to engage in violence,"[94] Huesmann states in a CNN Health online article. Based on many studies that link violent media and real-world violence, in 2013 Ohio State University psychology professor Brad Bushman wrote, "The overwhelming majority of social scientists working in the area now accept that media violence poses a danger to society."[95]

"The overwhelming majority of social scientists working in the area now accept that media violence poses a danger to society."[95]

— Ohio State University psychology professor and researcher Brad Bushman.

Personality and Aggression

However, numerous psychologists believe that studies that conclude that violent media cause aggression and violence fail to control for other factors, such as violence in the home and inborn tendencies toward violence. Studies by Stetson University psychologist Christopher J. Ferguson, for example, indicate that children who already have aggressive personalities are most likely to choose to play violent video games. When these children do commit violent acts, they may copy violent behavior they learned in these games. Ferguson thus concludes that "video game violence does not cause violent behavior but may have an impact on its form."[96] Ferguson also finds that the presence of mental illness or violence in the home, rather than the type of video games played, has the most influence on whether people born with violent tendencies will commit violent acts.

Psychologist Stanton E. Samenow agrees that whereas environmental influences may affect violent behavior, the root cause is inborn factors. Samenow writes in *Psychology Today*, "Violent tendencies reside within the personality, whether or not the person watches programming depicting violence. The television program, the movie, or the videogame do not turn him into something alien to his basic personality."[97] Samenow also notes that millions of people play violent video games, but the vast majority of them do not commit crimes.

> "Video game violence does not cause violent behavior but may have an impact on its form."[96]
>
> — Stetson University psychologist and researcher Christopher Ferguson.

Ongoing Challenges

As legal and behavior experts continue to untangle the factors that may influence crimes related to the Internet and digital devices, various solutions and strategies for containing these crimes have emerged. For example, since many view online anonymity as fueling Internet crimes, various ideas for ending online anonymity have been proposed. Many free-speech and privacy advocates, however, oppose ending Internet anonymity because they believe it would discourage political dissidents and crime victims from speaking out. In 2012, when New York lawmakers introduced legislation to ban anonymous posts on New York–based websites, attorney Kurt Opsahl stated, "The law is clearly unconstitutional. The right to speak anonymously is part of the First Amendment and has been since the founding of this country."[98]

Debates about solutions to problems fueled by digital technologies, along with controversies about the causes and implications of these problems, will no doubt continue in the future as society adjusts to the many positive and negative aspects of life in the digital age. The consensus that has emerged about these technologies is that it is important for digital device users to think about how these technologies are affecting themselves and society. That way, individuals can make informed decisions about whether they wish to allow smartphones to run their lives instead of controlling when and how they use these tools. As computer scientist Harrington writes in her book *Technology and Society*, "There are both good and bad aspects to just about everything we humans create, manufacture, and synthesize. Which way the balance tips for any given technology depends on how we use it."[99]

Facts

- Studies indicate that one-third of American teens have been a target of cyberbullying, and more than half know someone who has been a target.

- Studies show that video gaming is one of the most popular pastimes for adolescents, with about 97 percent of twelve- to seventeen-year-olds regularly playing video games on computers, consoles such as Wii or PlayStation, smartphones, Game Boy devices, and tablets.

- The Millennium Cohort Study by British researchers found that children born between 2000 and 2002 who spent more than three hours per day in front of a digital-device screen were more likely to engage in antisocial behavior, fighting, and stealing by age five.

- A 2011 study by Veriphyr found that more than 70 percent of health care providers had suffered patient privacy breaches by hackers. Provider employees were responsible for 35 percent of these illegal acts.

Source Notes

Introduction: Digital Devices: The Good, the Bad, and the Ugly

1. Quoted in Andy Campbell, "Texting Driver Who Slammed Cyclist: I, Like, 'Just Don't Care,'" *Huffington* Post, April 16, 2014. www.huffingtonpost.com.
2. Quoted in Campbell, "Texting Driver Who Slammed Cyclist."
3. Chris Matyszczyk, "'I Just Don't Care,' Says Texting Driver Who Hit Cyclist," CNET, April 15, 2014. www.cnet.com.
4. Richard Watson, *Future Minds*. London: Nicholas Brealey, 2010, p. 161.
5. Quoted in Cristen Conger, "Don't Blame Facebook for the Narcissism Epidemic," Discovery News, August 4, 2011. http://news.discovery.com.
6. Neil Postman, *Technopoly*. New York: First Vintage, 1993, p. xii.
7. Larry Rosen, *iDisorder*. New York: Palgrave MacMillan, 2012, pp. 5–6.
8. Eric Schmidt and Jared Cohen, *The New Digital Age: Reshaping the Future of People, Nations, and Business*. New York: Alfred A. Knopf, 2013, p. 11.

Chapter One: What Are the Origins of the Digital Device Controversies?

9. Everett M. Rogers, *Diffusion of Innovations*, 5th ed. New York: Free Press, 2003, p. xix.
10. William H. Davidow, *Overconnected: The Promise and Threat of the Internet*. Harrison, NY: Delphinium, 2011, p. 136.
11. Nancy Gibbs, "Your Life Is Fully Mobile," *Time*, August 16, 2012. http://techland.time.com.
12. Jane M. Healy, *Failure to Connect*. New York: Simon & Schuster, 1998, p. 27.
13. Sara Konrath, "The Empathy Paradox: Increasing Disconnection in the Age of Increasing Connection," in *Handbook of Research on Technoself: Identity in a Technological Society*, ed. Rocci Luppicini. Hershey, PA: IGI Global, 2013, p. 205.
14. Quoted in Bartleby.com, *Respectfully Quoted: A Dictionary of Quotations*. www.bartleby.com.
15. Quoted in Konrath, "The Empathy Paradox."
16. Quoted in Konrath, "The Empathy Paradox."
17. John Dowing, ed., *The SAGE Handbook of Media Studies*. Thousand Oaks, CA: SAGE, 2004, p. 185.
18. Dowing, ed., *The SAGE Handbook of Media Studies*, p. 186.
19. Dowing, ed., *The SAGE Handbook of Media Studies*, p. 186.
20. Quoted in Profiles in Science, "Television and Growing Up: The Impact of Televised Violence: Report to the Surgeon General, United States Public Health Service, 1972," National Library of Medicine. http://profiles.nlm.nih.gov.
21. Ellen Wartella and Nancy Jennings, "New Media: Interactivity Accentuates Similar Promises and Concerns," *Children and Computer Technology*, vol. 10, no. 2, Fall/Winter 2000. www.princeton.edu.
22. US Department of Justice, "Protecting Children Online," National Criminal Justice Referral Service, April 23, 1998. www.ncjrs.gov.

23. Susan Adams, "The Biggest Mistakes 20-Something Job Seekers Make," *Forbes*, August 2, 2012. www.forbes.com.

24. Christopher Muther, "Instant Gratification Is Making Us Perpetually Impatient," *Boston Globe*, February 2, 2013. www.bostonglobe.com.

25. Kali H. Trzesniewski and M. Brent Donnellan, "Rethinking 'Generation Me': A Study of Cohort Effects from 1976–2006," *Perspectives on Psychological Science*, vol. 5, no. 1, January 2010, pp. 69–70.

Chapter Two: How Are Digital Devices Impacting Privacy and Social Interaction?

26. Pew Research Center, "Teens and Technology 2013," March 13, 2013. www.pewinternet.org.

27. Quoted in Janna Anderson and Lee Rainie, "Main Findings: Teens, Technology, and Human Potential in 2020," Pew Internet & American Life Project, February 29, 2012. www.pewinternet.org.

28. Susan Tardanico, "Is Social Media Sabotaging Real Communication?," *Forbes*, April 30, 2012. www.forbes.com.

29. Tardanico, "Is Social Media Sabotaging Real Communication?"

30. Quoted in RW³ Culture Wizard, "The Challenges of Working in Virtual Teams: Virtual Teams Survey Report—2013." www.rw-3.com.

31. Michelle Kessler, "Fridays Go from Casual to E-mail-Free," *USA Today*, October 5, 2007. http://usatoday.com.

32. Quoted in RW³ Culture Wizard, "The Challenges of Working in Virtual Teams."

33. Watson, *Future Minds*, p. 118.

34. Stephen Marche, "Is Facebook Making Us Lonely?," *Atlantic*, May 2012. www.theatlantic.com.

35. Quoted in Marche, "Is Facebook Making Us Lonely?"

36. Schmidt and Cohen, *The New Digital Age*, p. 6.

37. Judith Wagner DeCew, "Connecting Informational, 4th Amendment and Constitutional Privacy," Information Ethics and Policy. http://infoethics.ischool.uw.edu.

38. Jonathan Krim, "Subway Fracas Escalates into Test of the Internet's Power to Shame," *Washington Post*, July 7, 2005. www.washingtonpost.com.

39. Quoted in Krim, "Subway Fracas Escalates into Test of the Internet's Power to Shame."

40. Quoted in Ben Jones, "Latest Tax Tool: Internet Shaming," *USA Today*, December 22, 2005. http://usatoday30.usatoday.com.

41. Quoted in *Daily Record*, "Prince George's New Nanny Named and Shamed as a Council Tax Dodge on Internet List," March 26, 2014, www.dailyrecord.co.uk.

42. Lisa Heffernan, "Oversharing: Why Do We Do It and How Do We Stop?," *Huffington Post*, December 4, 2013. www.huffingtonpost.com.

43. Lane Sutton, "5 Ways to Avoid Oversharing on Social Media," Mashable, August 25, 2012. http://mashable.com.

44. Susan Greenfield, "Facebook Home Could Change Our Brains," *Telegraph*, April 6, 2013. www.telegraph.co.uk.

45. Quoted in Chris Matyszczyk, "Zuckerberg: I Know That People Don't Want Privacy," CNET, January 10, 2010. www.cnet.com.

46. Irina Raicu, "Are Attitudes About Privacy Changing?," Santa Clara University. www.scu.edu.

Chapter Three: How Do Digital Devices Affect the Brain and Thought Processes?

47. Quoted in Judy Lin, "Research Shows That Internet Is Rewiring Our Brains," UCLA Newsroom, October 15, 2008. http://newsroom.ucla.edu.

48. Quoted in Anderson and Rainie, "Main Findings."

49. Daphne Bavelier et al., "Children, Wired: For Better and for Worse," *Neuron*, vol. 67, September 9, 2010, p. 692.

50. Bavelier et al., "Children, Wired," p. 693.

51. Quoted in Christopher Bergland, "Video Gaming Can Increase Brain Size and Connectivity," *The Athlete's Way* (blog), *Psychology Today*, October 31, 2013. www.psychologytoday.com.

52. Quoted in Michelle Trudeau, "Video Games Boost Brain Power, Multitasking Skills," National Public Radio, December 20, 2010. www.npr.org.

53. Greenfield, "Facebook Home Could Change Our Brains."

54. Quoted in Columbia University, "Study Finds That Memory Works Differently in the Age of Google," July 14, 2011. http://news.columbia.edu.

55. American Academy of Pediatrics, "Media and Children." www.aap.org.

56. Gary Small and Gigi Vorgan, "Is the Internet Killing Empathy?," CNN, February 18, 2011. www.cnn.com.

57. Quoted in *Hechinger Ed* (blog), "Are Texting, Multitasking Teens Losing Empathy Skills? Some Differing Views," *Hechinger Report*. http://hechingered.org.

58. Quoted in Matt Richtel, "Growing Up Digital, Wired for Distraction," *New York Times*, November 21, 2010. www.nytimes.com.

59. Watson, *Future Minds*, p. 3.

60. Quoted in Ulla G. Foehr, "Media Multitasking Among American Youth: Prevalence, Predictors and Pairings," Kaiser Family Foundation, December 2006. http://kaiserfamilyfoundation.files.wordpress.com.

61. Carol J. Scott, "From Multi-tasking to Mindful Tasking," *Huffington Post*, March 5, 2013. www.huffingtonpost.com.

62. Quoted in Richtel, "Growing Up Digital, Wired for Distraction."

63. Quoted in UCLA Department of Psychology, "Russell Poldrack: Multi-tasking Adversely Affects the Brain's Learning Systems," July 25, 2006. www.psych.ucla.edu.

64. Quoted in Amanda MacMillan, "12 Reasons to Stop Multitasking Now," Fox News, June 18, 2013. www.foxnews.com.

65. Quoted in National Public Radio, "Does Multitasking Lead to a More Productive Brain?," June 11, 2010. www.npr.org.

Chapter Four: How Do Digital Devices Affect Physical and Mental Health?

66. F.J. Zimmerman and J.F. Bell, "Associations of Television Content Type and Obesity in Children," *American Journal of Public Health*, vol. 100, no. 2, February 2010, p. 334.

67. Victoria J. Rideout et al., "Generation M2: Media in the Lives of 8- to 18-Year-Olds," Kaiser Family Foundation, January 2010. http://kaiserfamilyfoundation.files.wordpress.com.

68. Rosen, *iDisorder*, p. 157.

69. Jean M. Twenge and W. Keith Campbell, *The Narcissism Epidemic*. New York: Simon & Schuster, 2009, p. x.

70. Twenge and Campbell, *The Narcissism Epidemic*, p. x.

71. Quoted in Sadie F. Dingfelder, "Reflecting on Narcissism," American Psychological Association, February 2011. www.apa.org.

72. Quoted in Katherine Bindley, "Bullying and Suicide: The Dangerous Mistakes We Make," *Huffington Post*, February 8, 2012. www.huffingtonpost.com.

73. Gwenn Schurgin and Kathleen Clarke-Pearson, "Clinical Report—the Impact of Social Media on Children, Adolescents, and Families," *Pediatrics*. http://pediatrics.aappublications.org.

74. Larry Magid, "'Facebook Depression': A Nonexistent Condition," *Huffington Post*, March 30, 2011. www.huffingtonpost.com.

75. Quoted in BBC News, "'Internet Addiction' Linked to Depression, Says Study," February 3, 2010. http://news.bbc.co.uk.

76. Quoted in BBC News, "'Internet Addiction' Linked to Depression, Says Study."

77. Rosen, *iDisorder*, p. 4.

78. Quoted in K. Aleisha Fetters, "Do You Google Your Symptoms?," *Prevention*. www.prevention.com.

79. Ira Hyman, "Are You Addicted to Your Cell Phone?," *Mental Mishaps* (blog), *Psychology Today*, March 27, 2013. www.psychologytoday.com.

80. Rosen, *iDisorder*, p. 67.

81. Peter Gray, "Video Game Addiction: Does It Occur? If So, Why?," *Freedom to Learn* (blog), *Psychology Today*, February 2, 2012. www.psychologytoday.com.

82. Quoted in Maura Judkis, "*Words with Friends:* Alec Baldwin Gives the Addictive Game a Boost," *Washington Post*, December 7, 2011. www.washingtonpost.com.

Chapter Five: Do Digital Devices Promote Crime?

83. Jan L. Harrington, *Technology and Society*. Sudbury, MA: Jones and Bartlett, 2009, p. 161.

84. John Wagley, "FBI Details Cyber Sting," *Security Management*. www.securitymanagement.com.

85. Anne Polta, "Patient Privacy vs. the Urge to Snoop," Health Beat, June 8, 2012. http://healthbeat.areavoices.com.

86. Preet Bharara, "Asleep at the Laptop," *New York Times*, June 3, 2012. www.nytimes.com.

87. Steve Bennett, "Staying a Step Ahead," Symantec. www.symantec.com.

88. Quoted in Stephen Rex Brown, "Florida Teen Cleared of Cyberbullying Rebecca Sedwick to Suicide: 'I Did Nothing Wrong,'" *New York Daily News*, November 21, 2013. www.nydailynews.com.

89. Quoted in Michael Martinez, "'Charges in Rebecca Sedwick's Suicide Suggest 'Tipping Point' in Bullying Cases," CNN, October 28, 2013. www.cnn.com.

90. Quoted in Martinez, "Charges in Rebecca Sedwick's Suicide Suggest 'Tipping Point' in Bullying Cases."

91. Peter K. Smith and Georges Steffgen, eds., *Cyberbullying Through the New Media*. New York: Psychology, 2013, p. 194.

92. Azy Barak, ed., *Psychological Aspects of Cyberspace: Theory, Research, Applications*. Cambridge, UK: Cambridge University Press, 2008. p. 129.

93. T. Willoughby et al., "A Longitudinal Study of the Association Between Violent Video Game Play and Aggression Among Adolescents," *Developmental Psychology*, vol. 48, no. 4, July 2012, p. 1044.

94. Quoted in Anne Harding, "Violent Video Games Linked to Child Aggression," CNN Health, 2009. www.cnn.com.

95. Brad Bushman, "Why Do People Deny Violent Media Effects?," *Get Psyched!* (blog), *Psychology Today*, February 18, 2013. www.psychologytoday.com.

96. Christopher J. Ferguson et al., "Violent Video Games and Aggression: Causal Relationship or Byproduct of Family Violence and Intrinsic Violence Motivation?," *Criminal Justice and Behavior*, vol. 35, no. 3, March 2008, p. 315.

97. Stanton E. Samenow, "Watching Violence in the Media Does Not Cause Crime," *Inside the Criminal Mind* (blog), *Psychology Today*, February 24, 2012. www.psychologytoday.com.

98. Quoted in Alex Fitzpatrick, "Lawmakers Call for an End to Internet Anonymity," Mashable, May 23, 2012. http://mashable.com.

99. Harrington, *Technology and Society*, p. xiii.

Related Organizations and Websites

Berkman Center for Internet & Society
23 Everett St., 2nd Floor
Cambridge, MA 02138
phone: (617) 495-7547
website: http://cyber.law.harvard.edu

The Berkman Center for Internet & Society at Harvard University is a research center that studies the development, operation, challenges, and laws relating to cyberspace. Experts from the fields of sociology, psychology, communications, education, law, and computer science share insights and research to help the world understand and develop strategies for dealing with ongoing and emerging issues.

Center for Democracy & Technology (CDT)
1634 I St. NW, #1100
Washington, DC 20006
phone: (202) 637-9800
website: https://cdt.org

The CDT is a nonprofit organization that strives to protect freedom of expression and personal privacy on the Internet. It publishes information about events that affect these issues and lobbies governments to enact legislation to protect these rights.

Center for Safe and Responsible Internet Use
Internet Safety Project
3507 N. University Ave., Suite 175
Provo, UT 84604
website: www.internetsafetyproject.org

The Center for Safe and Responsible Internet Use promotes Internet safety education for children and teenagers. Internet safety expert Nancy Willard heads this organization. The website provides articles, reports, and videos relating to Internet safety.

Common Sense Media

650 Townsend, Suite 435
San Francisco, CA 94104
phone: (415) 863-0600
website: www.commonsensemedia.org

Common Sense Media is a nonprofit organization that provides information and advocacy concerning the impact of media on children. Its programs educate parents, teachers, and children about all types of media to promote responsible media choices and related legislation.

Digital Society

website: www.digitalsociety.org

The Digital Society is a nonprofit digital think tank that explores issues related to digital technologies. Its website features articles on various challenges presented by technology, written by experts in law, computer science, government, and social science.

Electronic Frontier Foundation (EFF)

815 Eddy St.
San Francisco, CA 94109
phone: (415) 436-9333
website: www.eff.org

The EFF is a nonprofit organization that defends civil liberties in the online world. It advises government personnel, educates the public, and provides legal and technological support to individuals and organizations threatened by security and privacy breaches and by challenges to free expression and innovation.

Federal Trade Commission (FTC)

600 Pennsylvania Ave. NW
Washington, DC 20580
phone: (202) 326-2222
website: www.ftc.gov

The FTC is a government agency that regulates business practices and protects and educates consumers. It also investigates and enforces laws relating to commerce, including issues concerning mobile technologies, Internet scams, and privacy violations.

Internet Education Foundation

1634 I St. NW
Washington, DC 20006
phone: (202) 638-4370
website: www.neted.org

The Internet Education Foundation is a nonprofit organization that educates the public about Internet-related issues and promotes informed Internet-related public policies. The foundation sponsors educational conferences and shares relevant news on its website.

Internet Society

1775 Wiehle Ave., Suite 201
Reston, VA 20190
phone: (703) 439-2120
website: www.internetsociety.org

The Internet Society is an international organization that strives for equal worldwide access to the Internet to benefit people everywhere. It provides information on Internet-related topics and sponsors projects designed to promote its mission.

Pew Research Center

1615 L St. NW, Suite 700
Washington, DC 20036
phone: (202) 419-4300
website: www.pewresearch.org

The Pew Research Center is a nonprofit, nonpartisan fact-gathering and research group that conducts social science research on current issues. Its Internet & American Life Project conducts surveys and publishes fact sheets about a variety of issues related to the Internet and other modern technologies.

Wired Safety

website: www.wiredsafety.org

Wired Safety is run by volunteers who provide information and support to others who have been affected by cybercrime or who seek information on Internet safety and privacy.

Additional Reading

Books

Nicholas Carr, *The Shallows: What the Internet Is Doing to Our Brains.* New York: W.W. Norton, 2010.

Brian X. Chen, *Always On: How the iPhone Unlocked the Anything-Anytime-Anywhere Future.* Cambridge, MA: Da Capo, 2012.

Howard Gardner and Katie Davis, *The App Generation: How Today's Youth Navigate Identity, Intimacy, and Imagination in a Digital World.* New Haven, CT: Yale University Press, 2013.

Andrew Keen, *Digital Vertigo: How Today's Online Social Revolution Is Dividing, Diminishing, and Disorienting Us.* New York: St. Martin's, 2012.

Larry Rosen, *iDisorder.* New York: Palgrave Macmillan, 2012.

Eric Schmidt and Jared Cohen, *The New Digital Age: Reshaping the Future of People, Nations, and Business.* New York: Alfred A. Knopf, 2013.

Sherry Turkle, *Alone Together: Why We Expect More from Technology and Less from Each Other.* New York: Basic, 2012.

Richard Watson, *Future Minds: How the Digital Age Is Changing Our Minds, Why This Matters, and What We Can Do About It.* London: Nicholas Brealey, 2010.

Internet Articles

Federal Communications Commission, "History of Communications." http://transition.fcc.gov/cgb/kidszone/history.html.

Perri Klass, "Seeing Social Media More as Portal than as Pitfall," *New York Times*, January 9, 2012. www.nytimes.com/2012/01/10/health/views/seeing-social-media-as-adolescent-portal-more-than-pitfall.html.

Barry M. Leiner et al., "Brief History of the Internet," Internet Society. www.internetsociety.org/internet/what-internet/history-internet/brief-history-internet#Origins.

National Crime Prevention Council, "Cyberbullying." www.ncpc.org/topics/cyberbullying.

Matt Richtel, "Digital Devices Deprive Brain of Needed Downtime," *New York Times*, August 24, 2010. www.nytimes.com/2010/08/25/technology/25brain.html?pagewanted=all&_r=0.

David Strom, "Be Careful Whom You Befriend on Social Networks," Internet Safety Project, November 5, 2011. www.internetsafetyproject.org/article/be-careful-whom-you-befriend-social-networks.

Taylor & Francis Online, "Does Your iPod Make You Socially Isolated?," *Science Daily*, February 26, 2014. www.sciencedaily.com/releases/2014/02/140226074833.htm.

Tarun Wadhwa, "Yes, You Can Hack a Pacemaker (and Other Medical Devices Too)," *Forbes*, December 6, 2012. www.forbes.com/sites/singularity/2012/12/06/yes-you-can-hack-a-pacemaker-and-other-medical-devices-too.

Index

Note: Boldface page numbers indicate illustrations.

3 1491 01175 3625

Niles
Public Library District
JUN 1 6 2015

Niles, Illinois 60714